30 days
to a more
powerful
prayer life

A PLAN TO TRANSFORM YOUR HEART AND YOUR WORLD

Joe Engelkemier

Pacific Press® Publishing Association
Nampa, Idaho
Oshawa, Ontario, Canada

Edited by Kenneth R. Wade
Designed by Michelle Petz

Copyright ©1998 by
Pacific Press® Publishing Association
Printed in the United States of America
All Rights Reserved

ISBN 0-8163-1648-1

98 99 00 01 02 • 5 4 3 2 1

Table of Contents

Foreword

In recent months and years we have seen an increased understanding of the power and absolute necessity of prayer in the life of the Christian. God's people everywhere are experiencing a new hunger for His presence in their lives. They are experiencing tremendous blessings from united and personal prayer.

We're seeing that prayer truly does kindle prayer and heart warms heart. In this book, Elder Joe Engelkemier helps us to see how we can deepen and enrich our lives and the lives of others through prayer. By interceding for others, our own love for Jesus and for others is intensified.

What a privilege to unite our prayers with those of Christ as He is praying for us and for our needs and identifying Himself with our prayer concerns. The truth of Hebrews 7:25 has been brought home beautifully in a wonderful gospel song by Carolyn Gillman that mentions that Jesus is "ever interceding" on our behalf.

In this book you'll find tools and wonderful truths and principles that will make your prayer life a joy and something you'll look forward to with eager expectation as you "come boldly to the throne" with your worship and requests.

Ruthie Jacobsen
Prayer Conference Coordinator

Introduction:
Your Prayers and the
New Millennium

What will you be doing the night that a new millennium begins?

Earlier you could have made plans to celebrate at the Rainbow Room in New York at $1,000 per person. But that's no longer an option; by the mid-1990s that glitzy party place had already stopped taking reservations, and Manhattan's Waldorf-Astoria hotel also was full.

If you belonged to the 6,000-member Millennium Society, you could have arranged something a little more in keeping with your faith. Ever since 1985 that group has been warming up for the night when one-nine-nine-nine will become two-zero-zero-zero. They celebrated New Year's Eve at the Great Wall of China in 1985 and at the Berlin Wall in 1989, with guests asked to bring a hammer and chisel. Plans for the end of 1999 include a ten-day cruise from New York to Alexandria, Egypt, to spend New Year's Eve at the Great Pyramid of Cheops, at Giza.

What do you most want from the rest of this millennium and the start of the next? Would you like to pray with more confidence and with greater power? Would you be pleased if your prayers and witness could hasten the return of Jesus?

You've probably noticed that December 31, 1999, comes on a Friday. The first day of the new millennium will be a Sabbath! Could that be providential? For Seventh-day Adventists, shouldn't January 1 of A. D. 2000 be a day of gratitude, reflection, and prayer?

"The power of prayer has never been tried to its full capacity in any church," said J. Hudson Taylor, the man who helped launch modern missions. "If we want to see mighty wonders of divine power and grace," he added, "let the whole church answer God's standing challenge, 'Call unto

Me, and I will answer thee, and show thee great and mighty things which thou knowest not' (Jer. 33:3, KJV)."

Seeking "great and mighty things"

As this millennium closes, the Seventh-day Adventist Church has an unprecedented opportunity to call upon the Lord to do mighty things. The August 2, 1997, issue of the Benton Harbor *Herald Palladium* included an article titled "Global Broadcast Set at Andrews." It summarized NET '98 like this:

> "A global satellite television series, designed to reach every continent, will originate from Andrews University's Pioneer Memorial Church in Berrien Springs during the fall of 1998.
>
> "The programs will be transmitted in 40 languages overseas and in English, Spanish, Portuguese, and French in North America.
>
> "Pioneer pastor Dwight Nelson has been chosen by the North American Division of Seventh-day Adventists to be the speaker for a live television program designed to appeal to all generations and especially to 'Generation X,' ages 13-33."

Forty languages! Every continent! How shall we go about mobilizing a revival of prayer? What will it take to get thousands of believers on their knees to seek the Lord? What kind of motivation will it take to get us to develop friendships with people we can invite to the meetings?

The Message and Mission theme selected for 1998—"Experience the Power of God's Word"—needs to be our purpose right into the next millennium. It's not just NET '98 that calls for much prayer backed with Scripture and by faith in the blood of Christ. Current movements toward revival through Bible study, prayer, and ministry indicate, I believe, that revival is about to spread until it pervades the work of God in every country on earth.

A morning worship discovery

For morning worship my wife and I have been reading from The Message, a paraphrased New Testament by Eugene H. Peterson. Yesterday we read the first seven verses of Acts 6, a passage about the selection of deacons. The New King James Version translates verse 4: "We will give ourselves continually to prayer and to the ministry of the word."

I love the way The Message tells the results of that prayer program: "The Word of God prospered. The number of disciples . . . increased dramatically." Or as verse 1 puts it, "by leaps and bounds."

The fact that membership increased so dramatically—twelve months after Calvary the 120 in the upper room had increased to more than twenty thousand—is evidence that giving prayer top priority during that year brought results. (See Acts 2:41, 4:4, 5:14, and 6:7 for a report of the events that took place during the twelve months following Pentecost.) All through the more than twenty years covered by Acts, in fact, prayer gets more mention than any other topic. There are two dozen references to prayer.

"Every great movement of God can be traced to a kneeling figure," Dwight L. Moody once declared. Will you join me in pleading that God will cause people of every age and race—Generation X people, midlife people, those approaching retirement, the elderly, even children—to joyfully increase their prayer time?

One remarkable development of the 1990s has been the growth of conferences that focus on new methods of prayer, of Bible study, and of ministry. At the time of this writing, 600 teens from across North America have just returned to their academies and churches after a prayer and ministry conference that took place on September 24-27, 1997, at Southwestern Adventist University.

That four days demonstrated that God is ready to work with unprecedented power in the hearts of Adventist youth. Ruthie Jacobsen, the North American Division prayer conference director, said that several of the adults present agreed that "there were literally hundreds of teens who accepted Christ either for the first time or in a more real way." As they left, several teens asked, "Why did this conference have to end so soon?"

My purpose in writing

This book, in part, is a testimony about my own experience over the last two years. It is my purpose:

1. To offer suggestions that can help readers find more joy and a greater effectiveness in intercessory prayer.

2. To recruit thousands who will pray for NET '98 and other evangelistic efforts as we approach and enter A. D. 2000.

3. To provide a tool that churches, youth leaders, women's ministry groups, schools, and even entire conferences can use to help develop Spirit-filled prayer, Bible study, and ministry groups.

4. To provide youth and adults who attend prayer and ministry conferences an aid they can take to their schools and churches, both for personal growth and for helping to get others enthused about prayer, Bible study, and ministry.

5. To encourage you to do all you can to build good relationships with the people you want to win to Christ.

Options to consider

As we go through the last two years of this millennium and into the next, this book can be read several different ways:

- One option would be to simply read it through like any other book, just to get information and inspiration.
- Over a thirty-day period read a chapter each day, and during that day use the closing suggestion or some other new insight that you gained from the chapter.
- Read a chapter and then spend two or three days thinking about and using key ideas.
- Take up to a week to assimilate each chapter and to test its suggestions.

Chapters begin with a Bible statement in bold print and close with an italicized suggestion or suggestions about how you might use one or more truths or ideas.

In the words of Dwight Nelson, let's "move forward on our knees." As we enter into heart-searching, repentance, and fervent prayer, may God do for us as Ephesians 3:20 promises: "Exceedingly abundantly above all that we ask or think."

1

So Much at Stake!

**"For the Son of Man has come
to seek and to save that which was lost" (Luke 19:10).**

The event: a skydiving jump from 12,000 feet.

Date and location: April 17, 1987, near Phoenix, Arizona.

The problem: a bloodied, unconscious young woman with an unopened parachute plunging toward a fatal impact.

On a blue-sky spring day Debbie Williams and half a dozen experienced skydivers had jumped, planning to link into a midair formation. A few seconds into her free-fall, Debbie went into a corkscrew, a fast dive to catch up with four others below her.

She miscalculated her descent and slammed into another diver. The fifty-mile-an-hour impact knocked her unconscious. She bounced away, limp as a rag doll.

The unconscious Debbie plummeted toward earth, her parachute unopened. As she fell past instructor and jumpmaster Gregory Robertson, he noticed the blood covering her face.

Immediately Gregory forced his body into a "no-lift" dive: head tucked into his chest, toes pointed, and arms flat at his side. Now he was diving at 180 miles an hour. As he looked down, Debbie still seemed to be far below him.

As the horizon rushed up to meet him, Gregory kept trying to dive faster, faster. He maneuvered his shoulders ever-so-slightly to guide his descent toward the unconscious young woman.

As he reached Debbie, he grabbed her reserve cord, yanked hard, then quickly moved away. Her chute opened, and she began drifting toward the ground. At 2,000 feet, twelve seconds from impact, Gregory opened his own chute.

Debbie recovered from her injuries—forever grateful to the one who had snatched her from a fatal impact.

You as the jump master

Imagine yourself as Gregory. As soon as you saw Debbie's bloodied face and unopened parachute, you would have known she was plunging toward certain death. Doubtless you, too, would have gone into a fast dive with a prayer that you could catch up with her and somehow grab her parachute cord.

We may not have thought of it that way, but if a friend or a family member is apart from Christ, isn't he or she headed toward a destiny just as fatal as Debbie's could have been?

One report indicates that in Europe's increasingly secular society "Christendom loses 50-75 percent of its young people to the world." The same could probably be said for North America, where an estimated one million people raised in Adventist homes no longer attend church.

God yearns for these missing ones to be brought back to Him. He wants all of us to so earnestly seek Him that He can give us large amounts of His Holy Spirit. He longs to pour out unprecedented blessings on our attempts to take the "eternal gospel"—the messages of Revelation 14—"to every nation, tribe, tongue, and people" (Rev. 14:6).

The wonders of the gospel

I grew up with almost no knowledge of Jesus Christ. I don't recall ever seeing a Bible until I found one in a closet when in my early teens. Then through the influence of the *Voice of Prophecy* I was baptized, just before turning 17. The simplicity of the plan God uses to save us can be summed up in this one sentence: "He made Him who knew no sin to be sin for us, that we might become the righteousness of God in Him" (2 Cor. 5:21).

That's a transaction! I give Christ my sinful heart, and He gives me His righteousness. *Steps to Christ* expresses the same truth like this: "If you give yourself to Him, and accept Him as your Saviour, then, sinful as your life may have been, for His sake you are accounted righteous" (62).

The next sentence declares: "Christ's character stands in place of your character, and you are accepted before God just as if you had not sinned" (ibid.).

That truth brings fantastic blessings—benefits few have fully grasped. Here's one: It can increase the boldness and faith with which we pray. In another place the same author says:

As we approach God through the virtue of Christ's merits we are clothed with His priestly vestments. He places us close by His side, encircling us with His human arm, while with His divine arm He grasps the throne of the Infinite. He puts His merits as sweet incense in a censer in our hands in order to encourage our petitions (*In Heavenly Places*, 77).

Have you heard it put that way? We can pray clothed with Christ's priestly garments! I'd like to suggest that this is especially true as we pray for NET '98 and other attempts to share the gospel during the last two years of this millennium.

There's so much at stake! In the same book Ellen White suggests, "Educate yourself to have unlimited confidence in God" (71). As we progress we'll share "how-to" suggestions. But everything begins with appropriating the righteousness of Christ.

One time in a Bible class a teacher asked a little fellow, "Son, is there anything God can't do?" The little fellow thought for a moment then replied, "Yes, He cannot see my sins through the blood of Jesus."

In intercessory prayer so much is at stake! Through faith in Christ's blood we can boldly ask for God to work through His Spirit in the hearts and lives of others. We can plead, "Do whatever it takes to bring them to the foot of the Cross."

What *is* at stake?

The best-known and most loved of all Bible statements is John 3:16, with its promise of eternal life through choosing Jesus as Saviour. In my religion classes I often try to illustrate the word *eternal* by taking a pint jar of sand and slowly pouring it into a dish. As the tens of thousands of grains trickle down, I suggest that students think of each grain of sand as representing a year of eternity.

One time when I did this, a chemistry student said, "Let me take that pint of sand to the chemistry lab, and I'll try to find out approximately how many grains of sand it contains." When he returned the jar, he had written this on the lid: about 1,100,000 grains.

It was at a beach of Lake Michigan that I came up with the preceding illustration. While there, I had asked myself, "If every grain of sand on Lake Michigan's more than four hundred miles of beaches symbolizes a year of eternity, how much time would be represented just by the sand around Lake Michigan? And if you add Australia's 14,000 miles of beaches . . . ? And all of South America's . . . ?

To close the illustration, I turn to Mark 8:36, 37 and read these two questions of Jesus: "What will it profit a man if he gains the whole world, and loses his own soul? Or what will a man give in exchange for his soul?"

Here are two suggestions as you think about the truths of this first chapter:

- *Make a mental note of the sand illustration; then the next time you are at the beach, pick up a handful of sand. As you let it trickle through your fingers, share the above thoughts with a family member or friend.*
- *If God speaks to you through anything in this chapter, write two or three sentences or quotations on a 3 by 5 card, and during the day keep coming back to and praying about what you have written.*

2

More and More and Still More!

**"This I pray, that your love may abound still more
and more in knowledge and all discernment" (Phil. 1:9).**

"Do you ever worry about whether or not it will get dark in the evening or whether dawn will return the next morning?" It's a foolish question. But sometimes I ask it anyway in my Workshop in Prayer classes. I then point out that in the return of dawn and dusk is a twice-a-day reminder of the certainty of God's promises.

As a class we turn to Jeremiah 33 and underline this assurance:

> Thus says the Lord, "If you can break My covenant with the day and My covenant with the night, so that there will not be day and night in their season, then My covenant may also be broken with David my servant, so that he shall not have a son to reign on his throne" (Jer. 33:20, 21).

That promise became a reality when Jesus, the Son of David, was born. Isaiah had predicted, "Of the increase of His government and peace there will be no end, upon the throne of David and over His kingdom" (Isa. 9:7).

Most years since the early 1970s I have taught "Workshop in Prayer" classes at Andrews University. As books, I currently use *Incredible Answers to Prayer,* by Roger Morneau and my own *Whatever It Takes Praying.* We also underline eighty Old Testament and eighty New Testament promises, plus fifty command-promises. We find that using Bible promises as we pray helps increase our faith.

Using Bible prayers

In 1996, as I sought to increase my own effectiveness in prayer, I began using some of Paul's prayers in my own prayers. I started with this one:

> This I pray, that your love may abound still more and more in knowledge and all discernment, that you may approve the things that are excellent, that you may be sincere and without offense till the day of Christ, being filled with the fruits of righteousness which are by Jesus Christ, to the glory and praise of God (Phil. 1:9-11).

I wrote the above on a 3 by 5 card to help me memorize the text. (I changed the pronouns to *him* or *her* or to *them* or *their*.) I then began—when walking, driving, or whatever—to pray this as a prayer for Adventist youth.

Paul's petition takes in just about every spiritual need anyone could have:

- More love, both for Christ and for people
- The discernment—the eyesalve of Revelation 3:18—needed in decision making so as to choose not merely the good, but *the excellent*
- Readiness for the return of Christ
- Becoming filled with the fruits of the Spirit

In August 1996 I went to the room where I would be teaching my Workshop in Prayer class and prayed Philippians 1:9-11 for all who would register. Sometimes I would invite students to kneel with me, with the suggestion that several pray out loud. Often three or four students would pray with such sincerity that moisture would fill my eyes.

Selecting prayers to use

Paul's writings contain several of his prayers, and the psalms are filled with prayers that we can incorporate into our own praying. It isn't necessary, of course, to memorize a prayer passage to use it. One can, for example, open to a prayer of adoration, such as Psalm 92:1-5, and read it to the Lord before bringing requests to Him. I have found, however, that once a prayer is memorized I can use it many times a day just as part of my coming and going.

Let me close this chapter with these suggestions:

- *In your Bible underline Jeremiah 33:20, 21. Then at dawn and dusk try to make it a habit to thank God that in the natural world He gives a twice-a-day reminder of His dependability.*
- *Write out Philippians 1:9-11 on a 3 by 5 card and begin to include it in your petitions by using the card. As you become more familiar with it, you will gradually have it memorized.*

3

A Self-Check for Intercessors

**"I exhort first of all that supplications, prayers,
intercessions, and giving of thanks be made for all men,
for . . . [God] desires all men to be saved
and to come to the knowledge of the truth" (1 Tim. 2:1, 4).**

One survey indicated that Christians in North America were spending about three minutes a day in prayer. And the average pastor? About seven minutes.

What would a survey of Adventist believers and pastors show?

God invites us to join Him in "heavenly places" (Eph. 1:3) as we pray. By faith we can go there, clothed with Christ's priestly garments, to bring our requests. Are we doing so? As a checkup on how you are doing, both in Bible study and in intercessory prayer, consider these questions:

- Do you enjoy the study of God's Word so much that you feel like Job when he said, "I have treasured the words of His mouth more than my necessary food" (Job 23:12)?
- Do you focus on specific Bible promises as you pray? Have you found them, as Peter puts it in 2 Peter 1:4, to be "exceedingly great and precious"?
- In your praying do you approach God's throne with eager delight?
- Are you regularly getting decided answers to prayer?
- Have you tried intermingling some of the prayers of David, Paul, and other Bible writers into your prayers when you intercede for others?
- Do you pray with the confidence that every sincere prayer backed by faith in Christ's blood has an influence for good?

- Do you have occasions during group prayers when you sense God's Spirit so powerfully that you struggle to hold back tears of repentance and joy?

As we progress through this book we will have suggestions that may help you to answer a resounding Yes to many of the preceding questions.

Destinies at stake

As I tried to illustrate in chapter 1, there's a lot at stake when you pray! Your prayers can make a full-of-wonder difference in your own life and in the lives of the people for whom you have concerns. Prayer can also markedly increase the influence of events like NET '98.

During the 1,000 years after Christ comes, we will have opportunity to examine heaven's records. At that time you will find that every prayer backed by the merits of Christ will have had an influence for good. (More about this in chapter 6.) I am convinced, further, that one of our joys in eternity will be fellowship with those whose destinies have been affected by our intercessions in their behalf!

Think of someone—family member, friend, acquaintance—who has left Christ or who has not given himself or herself to Christ. For a moment see his or her face. What kind of future do you visualize for this person if he or she remains separated from Christ?

Paul is brutally blunt: "The wages of sin is death" (Rom. 6:23). All of us are sinners, and sin pays wages. You can't refuse the paycheck. I can't. The person whose face you have pictured can't.

If I'm apart from Christ when He comes, the final installment of my "pay" includes the "second death," described in Revelation 20. At the end of the millennium all the lost will live again to face the judgment. Satan himself will be there, and eventually he will be able to organize the lost billions—tyrants, murderers, adulterers, the rejecters of God's grace—into an army.

On D-day, as the assembled troops move forward into attack positions, God's throne appears above the city. The books are opened, the judgment takes place, and sentence is pronounced. Scripture tells what will happen next: "Fire came down from God out of heaven and devoured them" (Rev. 20:9).

Another option

In Romans 6:23 Paul also tells about an alternative: "The gift of God is eternal life." No pen can describe the wonder and joy of that gift, but let me try by asking, "What will you be doing a million years from today?"

You'll have done a lot of traveling by then and will have a good start on seeing the wonders of an endless universe. You'll have a perfect memory, so you won't get confused as to whom you met where.

You'll have perfect health. Revelation 21 declares that there will be no more pain or death (v. 4). As a son of God you will have Adam's stature by then. You'll be good looking and physically stronger than you would have ever dreamed possible. Best of all, you'll reflect the character qualities of Christ.

As a daughter of God you'll be a picture of feminine loveliness. But more wonderful, you will have been absorbing "still more and more" of the matchless attractions of Christ.

That's still future. But through reflecting Christ in the here and now, you can make a life-or-death difference in the lives of those who have left Christ or never known Him. Pray about these last two verses of James, as worded in Eugene Peterson's The Message paraphrase:

"My dear friends, if you know people who have wandered off from God's truth, don't write them off. Go after them. Get them back, and you will have rescued precious lives from destruction and prevented an epidemic of wandering away from God."

Here's suggestions for this third chapter:

- *Read Revelation 20 and the first eight verses of Revelation 21. The final chapter of* The Great Controversy *gives vivid details that will make the scenes more real to you.*
- *See yourself watching from inside the New Jerusalem as the assault of Revelation 20:9 takes place. What will be your feelings if there are people standing at your side who were influenced by your prayers to choose Christ?*
- *Reflect for a moment on the above paraphrased words of James; then use a 3 by 5 card to make a list of two or more people whom you know who have "wandered off from God's truth." Keep it in your Bible and pray often that God will use NET '98 or some other means to bring them back to Christ.*

4

Welcome to the White House (of the Universe)

"But God, who is rich in mercy, for His great love wherewith He loved us, even when we were dead in sins, hath quickened us together with Christ . . . and hath raised us up together, and made us sit in heavenly places in Christ Jesus" (Eph.2:4-6, KJV).

Would you like to develop a friendship with the most powerful person on earth? Or how about with the most wealthy?

Currently the most powerful person is President Bill Clinton. The wealthiest is Bill Gates. Would you like to become one of their close friends? And if so, would you like to have private phone numbers that would give you instant access?

There's probably zero chance for such friendships. But would you believe it? God offers something a hundred times better, friendship with Himself and instant access to Him at any time.

Paul's letter to the Ephesians has been called his "prayer epistle." It has two of his actual prayers (Eph. 1:15-23 and 3:14-19), one of which we will examine in a later chapter.

In heavenly places

I ask each student in my Workshop in Prayer class to get a copy of the devotional book *In Heavenly Places,* by Ellen G. White, so that for the ten weeks of the quarter they can get into the habit of reading a page each day. It is the most underlined of all my books, with one or more statements marked on almost every page.

The January 1 reading uses the Ephesians 2:4-6 text as the Bible statement. Of those who choose Christ it says: "They sit together in heavenly places in Christ, enjoying in communion with Him the joy and peace that He alone can give. They love Him with heart and mind and soul and strength, realizing they are His blood-bought heritage" (7).

Do any of us fully realize what *sitting together with Christ in heavenly places* means? Through faith we can sit at His side when we bring our petitions to the Father!

In Ephesians 6 Paul told of our need for "the whole armor of God" and urged that "above all" we take "the shield of faith" (16). Compare Paul with this from *In Heavenly Places*: "Let us have more confidence in our Redeemer. . . . Have faith in God. Trustful dependence on Jesus makes victory not only possible but certain" (17).

With Christ at His throne now!

In his book *Mighty Prevailing Prayer,* Wesley Duewel has a chapter entitled "Your Welcome to the Throne." He reminds us that God gives us "constant, instant access" to His throne and suggests that we remember that in prayer we are approaching the Sovereign of the universe. He then adds, "On the other hand, you should always remember how loved you are, how awaited and constantly welcome. You disappoint your heavenly Father if you do not come often and with freedom" (44, 45).

In condensed form, these are four of the truths about going to God's throne in prayer that Pastor Duewel presents:

1. Remember that you are approaching a throne of grace. God is "the God of all grace" (1 Peter 5:10). Twelve times the Bible speaks of "the grace of our Lord Jesus Christ."

2. Approach the throne with confident boldness (Heb. 4:16). The word *boldness* in Hebrews 4:16 means "freedom, unreservedness of speech; the absence of fear in speaking boldly."

3. Approach God in faith (Heb. 11:6). Remember that a throne is a place where decisions are made and where requests are granted.

4. Approach the throne with love and joy. Duewel puts it like this: "Approach . . . with love burning and glowing in your heart for Jesus, for His kingdom, and for those you pray for" (46).

He then adds, "Approach the throne with eager joy. You are asking for things God longs to do. . . . Your prayer time is always a joy time to the Lord" (ibid.).

Two prayers of Paul that I have memorized—Ephesians 3:14-19 and Colossians 1:9-13 begin with "For this reason." In Ephesians the reason is stated in 3:12—we "have boldness and access" through faith in Christ. In

Colossians 1 the reason seems to be that God's Word had already made them fruit bearers (6). At times I introduce these and other prayers with "For *these* reasons" and mention those that Pastor Duewel points out.

God is your Father, and when you address Him as Father, your requests are "music in His ears" (*Christ's Object Lessons*, 142). He is especially delighted when your requests are for the above-mentioned kingdom needs rather than just for personal benefits. In the words of Duewel, in going to God's throne "you are a kingdom official on kingdom business."

God's intense interest in you

In the context of our concern for material needs, Jesus said, "Seek first the kingdom of God and His righteousness, and all these things [food, clothes, etc.] shall be added to you" (Matt. 6:33). In that wonderful chapter in *Steps to Christ* called "The Privilege of Prayer," Ellen White points out that God takes "an immediate interest" in our every need, our every joy, our every perplexity (100).

And for your spiritual needs, could I suggest a two-sentence statement from *Messages to Young People* to use personally and to share when possible:

Nothing is apparently more helpless, yet really more invincible, than the soul that feels its nothingness, and relies wholly on the merits of the Saviour. God would send every angel in heaven to the aid of such an one, rather than allow him to be overcome (94).

Here's two possible uses for chapter 4 content:

- *The "music in your ears" statement comes from a chapter in* Christ's Object Lessons *titled "Asking to Give," which is commentary on Christ's remarks about prayer in Luke 11:1-13. For enrichment, take extra time and read both Luke 11:1-13 and "Asking to Give."*
- *This will require a little memory time, but if God so leads you, write out all four of Pastor Duewel's suggestions on a 3 by 5 card. Then begin at least some of your prayers with "For these reasons." You could reword his four reasons as praise and thank God that His throne is a throne of grace,that He invites you to come boldly, etc.*

5

Putting Delight Into Your Devotions

**"Your words were found, and I ate them,
and Your word was to me the joy
and rejoicing of my heart" (Jer. 15:16).**

In October 1996, forty students from Shenandoah Valley Academy (SVA) attended a Columbia Union Prayer Conference held at Mount Vernon Academy and upon their return established Bible study and prayer groups at their school. The September 6, 1997, issue of *Insight* included testimonies from SVA students that were largely the result of what happened at the prayer conference:

Joshua Haley, 16: "I really have a burden to serve God. I'm excited about Him like I've never been before."

Merrie Rennard, 16: "I've felt God lead me personally to SVA, where my spiritual life has grown by leaps and bounds."

Alice Wilson, 17: "Prayer groups give me a personal relationship with God. I know that daily time with Him is important, and each day I'm closer to being with Jesus."

Jessica Wade, 18: "I want to go to heaven because I'm in love with Christ, and I want to be with Him always."

Andrea Kuntaraf, 16: "Prayer groups have . . . broken down a lot of cliques, and now I'm able to talk about Jesus to people I never really talked to last year."

The first session among Adventists, called a prayer conference, took place in Oregon in 1988. There were two in 1990, three in 1991, thirteen in 1995, sixty-five in 1996, and more than eighty-five in 1997. As the numbers increased, the movement needed leadership, and in 1995 Ruthie Jacobsen was asked to direct such conferences in North America. Several have been primarily for teens and are called teen prayer and ministry conferences.

A prayer conference offers experience in three areas: prayer, Bible study, and ministry—all within the context of small groups. At the 1996 Mt. Vernon Conference, Spring Valley Academy, from Dayton, Ohio, provided the student leaders.

In April 1995 Spring Valley Academy had sent eight students to England, where nearly ninety other youth from North America conducted prayer conferences in the South England Conference. Upon their return God used the Spring Valley youth who had gone to bring a renewal on their own campus.

Delinda Snyder, an academy senior during the England trip and now at Andrews University, said this about what happened at Spring Valley after those who went to England had returned: "God led us to start a Friday night study group that grew from about a dozen to sixty students. Four students decided to be baptized, and God totally changed our school, so that you would see students talking about Christ and stopping to pray with each other in classrooms and in the hall."

Something similar happened at Shenandoah Valley when the forty students from there returned home after the October 1996 prayer conference at Mount Vernon. Students formed study groups they call the Timothy Club. *Insight* reported:

> To be a part of Timothy, the members have agreed to have half-hour personal devotions every day and come to lead prayer groups each evening. Then every Friday at 5:15 p.m. this group meets with Pastor Tom, and together they enjoy a short prayer time, an hour-long Bible study, a closing prayer, and then a discussion of upcoming activities and events.

That's balance! Time for personal devotion *and* group study. Love for Jesus enhances both kinds of experiences.

Our awesome Saviour

We'll tell more about the prayer and Bible study methods used at Prayer and Ministry Conferences in chapter 13. First, we want to focus on Jesus. What does it take to fall in love with Him?

Jesus said, "And I, if I am lifted up from the earth, will draw all peoples to Myself" (John 12:32). As I think about the awfulness of crucifixion, I wonder, "Why would Jesus—the Co-Creator of the galaxies—do that for me?"

When I first read *The Desire of Ages,* the chapter entitled "Calvary" gripped me. During my freshman year at what was then Southwestern Junior College, I memorized this sentence:

The spotless Son of God hung upon the cross, His flesh lacerated with stripes; those hands so often reached out in blessing, nailed to the wooden bars; those feet so tireless on ministries of love, spiked to the tree; that royal head pierced by the crown of thorns, those quivering lips shaped to the cry of woe (755).

I tried to picture what this sentence described, and my heart melted. Pause with me and ask yourself, "If I had been present that day, what would I have seen? What would I have heard? What would I have felt?"

I went on to then memorize this next sentence:

And all that He endured—the blood drops that flowed from His head, His hands, His feet, the agony that racked His frame, and the unutterable anguish that filled His soul at the hiding of His Father's face—speaks to each child of humanity, declaring, It is for thee that the Son of God consents to bear this burden of guilt; for thee He spoils the domain of death, and opens the gates of Paradise (ibid.).

He suffered all that for *me!* And for *you!* There on that cross *He opened the gates of Paradise.* And He would have done it for me alone, for you alone!

More reasons to love Him

There must be ten thousand more reasons to love Jesus. Here I can mention only one more: His full-of-wonder personality.

"Think of the kindest, strongest, most generous, and appealing person you have ever known," Norval Pease once wrote. "Then in your imagination magnify, purify, and enrich that individual a thousand times. Even so, you have not even begun to imagine what Jesus is like" ("What Jesus Can Do for You," *These Times,* Aug. 1981, 16).

What will it be like someday to sit with Him, along with friends, on the grass next to the River of Life? What will it be to see in His eyes love for you? What will it be to travel with Him to visit distant galaxies? On those trips, what will it be to give your testimony to unfallen beings?

Even now, Jesus Christ brings so much joy into the lives of His friends! "I don't call you servants," He said. "I call you My friends" (see John 15:15). It will take all of eternity to experience all the things Jesus wants to do for us!

Private Bible study

Here are suggestions for getting the most out of your private Bible study time and your prayer time:

1. Get adequate sleep. In order to be fresh and alert, most people need seven or eight hours of sleep. For those still in school the book *Education* suggests, "Since the work of building up the body takes place during the hours of rest it is essential, especially in youth, that sleep be regular and abundant" (205).

2. Get into the habit of underlining as you read the Bible; then use an underlined statement as "subject matter for prayer." Using Bible content helps eliminate dullness and sameness in prayer. I try to not just read or quote a verse or passage when in prayer but to use it as a basis to talk freely to God about what it says.

3. When weather and surroundings permit, go out-of-doors for some of your appointments with Jesus. Yesterday I rode my bicycle to a cornfield. I prayed, mostly aloud, while riding, and then knelt in the cornfield to pray.

Try it if at all possible. In the words of another, "Let the fresh glories of each new morning awaken praise in your heart for these tokens of His loving care" (*Testimonies for the Church*, 5:312).

4. Develop an interest in God's work throughout the world and pray especially for our schools and for Adventist youth in public schools. The Bible repeatedly makes statements like this: "All the ends of the earth shall see the salvation of our God" (Isa. 52:10). In volume 4 of the *Testimonies*, Ellen White suggests: "The varied interests of the cause furnish us with food for reflection and inspiration for our prayers" (459).

If you get *The Adventist Review*, scan it to learn of a region or group that would benefit from your intercession in their behalf. You could do the same with your Union paper.

5. Try to make it a habit to breathe praises and prayers to God in your coming and going. "Pray without ceasing, "Paul urged (1 Thess. 5:17). *The Ministry of Healing* gives a suggestion about how to do so:

> It is not always necessary to bow upon your knees to pray. Cultivate the habit of talking with the Saviour when you are alone, when you are walking, and when you are busy with your daily labor. Let the heart be continually uplifted in silent petitions for help, for light, for strength, for knowledge. Let every breath be a prayer (510, 511).

To use this chapter's content consider these options:

- *Copy one of the two sentences cited in this chapter from* The Desire of Ages *onto a 3 by 5 card and use it as you pray to thank Jesus for what He did on the cross.*
- *Review the suggestions for adding delight to your devotional times. Then select one that would be a new experience for you and try it for a week. Make a new habit out of it.*
- *Start using the expression "still more and more" (Phil. 1:9) as you ask for the above-mentioned help, light, strength, and knowledge.*

6

Awesome Truths About Prayer

"Finally, brethren, pray for us, that the word of the Lord may have free course and be glorified, just as it is with you" (2 Thess. 3:1).

The *Guinness Book of World Records* relates that in 1958 Mrs. Deborah Schneider of Minneapolis wrote 25 words to complete a sentence in a contest for the best blurb for Plymouth cars. She won $500 a month for life. With normal life expectations, she would collect $12,000 per word.

That would be an awesome recompense!

We don't think of getting "paid" by the word when we plead with God for the salvation of others. But could it be that every petition will bring a recompense far in excess of $12,000 per word?

In studying and teaching about prayer I've found several truths about intercession for hurting and lost people that I see as awesome. These include:

1. In answer to our intercessory prayers, angels perform a ministry they otherwise would not carry out.

In speaking of angels Paul asked, "Are they not all ministering spirits sent forth to minister for those who will inherit salvation?" (Heb. 1:14). And in a passage about prayer for the sick, James requested, "Pray for one another, that you may be healed" (James 5:16). As a comment, note this: "When you neglect to pray for the sick, you deprive them of great blessings, for angels of God are waiting to minister to these souls in response to your petitions" (*Medical Ministry*, 195).

Do we find support for this idea in the realities of daily life? The March 1996 issue of *Reader's Digest* printed a story by Larry Dossey, M.D., entitled

"Can Prayer Heal?" Dr. Dossey told of an experiment with heart patients in a San Francisco hospital who were prayed for by an anonymous group of petitioners and of another group who were not prayed for. Here's how those prayed for benefited:

- They were five times less likely than the unremembered group to require antibiotics.
- They were two and a half times less likely to suffer congestive heart failure.
- They were less likely to suffer cardiac arrest.

I'm confident God and the angels are just as concerned about spiritual ills as for physical ailments. For my Workshop in Prayer class I paraphrase the *Medical Ministry* statement like this:

> When you neglect to pray for a non-Christian friend or a family member who is spiritually weak, you deprive that individual of great blessings, for angels of God are waiting to minister to these individuals in response to your petitions!

What do you think? If you have family and friends who are spiritually ill, could it be that angels are waiting to minister in response to *your petitions*? Through prayer, compassion, and tact could you make a life-changing difference as you reach out to them?

2. Not a single sincere prayer is ever lost; each has an influence for good.

"Therefore I say to you," Jesus told the disciples, "whatever things you ask when you pray, believe that you receive them, and you will have them" (Mark 11:24). The context enlarges on two conditions, faith and a forgiving spirit (see Mark 11:22-26). And as we note in chapter 15, other conditions are mentioned elsewhere in Scripture.

Someone has said, "We pray not to get what we want, but to find out what God wants." To find His will, we go to the Word of God. As we follow its instructions, we can know that every sincere prayer is heard and will be answered according to God's will and in His timing. The author of *Christ's Object Lessons* makes this encouraging statement:

> Never is one repulsed who comes to Him with a contrite heart. Not one sincere prayer is lost. . . . We pour out our heart's desire in our closets, we breathe a prayer as we walk by the way, and our words reach the throne of the Monarch of the universe. . . . It is God to whom we are speaking, and our prayer is heard (*Christ's Object Lessons*, 174).

3. The final results of every sincere prayer are recorded upon "heaven's

imperishable records," and in eternity one of our joys will be fellowship with people blessed by our prayers.

Jesus taught that every idle word is recorded (Matt. 12:36, 37). Malachi wrote that the words of "those who feared the Lord" and "spoke to one another" are all written in "a book of remembrance" (Mal. 3:16).

Do you see what that means? Every petition that you and I have prayed will be on the record books of heaven for all eternity. That's a sobering thought for those days when my prayers are few! But it's also an encouragement to pray more and to ask for more.

In the Sermon on the Mount Jesus urged, "Lay up for yourselves treasures in heaven" (Matt. 6:20). At one time I thought that statement had to do mostly with funds we give to win people to Christ. Then I asked myself, "If my prayers can help bring people to Christ, am I not also laying up treasure in heaven through intercessory prayer in behalf of others?"

At times I have taught a class at Andrews in which we survey the nine volumes of *Testimonies for the Church*. As I prepared a syllabus I discovered this: "I was shown that the recording angel makes a faithful record of every offering dedicated to God and put into the treasury, and also of the final result of the means thus bestowed" (2:518).

Heaven records every offering and then keeps track of *the final result of the means thus bestowed!* Now add: "Every act of love, every word of kindness, every prayer in behalf of the suffering and oppressed, is reported before the eternal throne and placed on heaven's imperishable record" (5:133).

Could it be that the final results of each prayer are also recorded? And if so, will those blessed through your prayers want to search you out and thank you? That alone should be incentive to do a lot of praying!

As you reflect upon the content of this chapter, may I suggest two possible applications from which to choose:

- *Take a 3 by 5 card and write Hebrews 1:14 and the statement from page 195 of* Medical Ministry *cited at the start of this chapter. Then as you pray for people who are physically or spiritually ill, thank God for the difference your prayers and the ministry of angels can make.*
- *Just before Paul was beheaded, he wrote Timothy, "Without ceasing I remember you in my prayers night and day" (2 Tim. 1:3). Eugene Peterson's* The Message *paraphrase has Paul saying, "Every time I say your name in prayer—which is practically all the time—I thank God for you." You could write Paul's statement on a 3 by 5 card and then list a dozen or more family or friends on it. Keep the card in your Bible, and as you open your Bible take a few moments to pray for the people you've listed.*

7

What Would Happen If . . . ?

"Your word I have hidden in my heart" (Ps. 119:11).

Did you know that Jonah's prayer from the belly of the whale included several expressions from the psalms and that Mary's ten-verse prayer in Luke 1:46-55 includes thoughts from no less than eighteen Old Testament passages?

Apparently it was common in Bible times to include Bible phrases and passages when you were praying. I find that doing this while praying increases my sense of expectation. It helps me move toward the kind of faith described here: "Educate yourself to have unlimited confidence in God" (*In Heavenly Places*, 71).

In chapter 2 I told of starting to use the following prayer of Paul when praying for the youth of the church:

> And this I pray, that your love may abound still more and more in knowledge and all discernment, that you may approve the things that are excellent, that you may be sincere and without offense till the day of Christ, being filled with the fruits of righteousness by Jesus Christ to the glory and praise of God (Phil. 1:9-11).

For more than a year I have used this prayer many times a day. As others join in doing so, our expectation is that increasing numbers of the youth of the church will develop:

An experience that abounds with more and still more love for Christ. Only love lastingly motivates a young person or anyone to give himself or herself fully to

Christ. Paul tells us how that love grows: by beholding Christ (2 Cor. 3:18).

An increased love for people. A prominent theme of 1 John is this: God is love. And here's a second focus: The fruit of our love for God is a love for people and an increased desire to help people.

An experience in which discernment is strong. The Laodiceans of Revelation 3:18 urgently need eye slave—the discernment that can detect sin under even the most attractive disguise. And never in history have youth more desperately needed such discernment. Ancient Israel demanded a king, that they "might be like all the nations" (1 Sam. 8:20). A desire to be like everybody ruined God's plans for His Old Testament people and continues to do untold damage to the witness of the Seventh-day Adventist Church.

What brings the discernment that rejects the poison of this deadly inclination? Isn't it eyes fixed on a crucified Saviour? Perhaps that's why we need to spend some time in the Gospels or books like *The Desire of Ages* every day.

An ability to choose the things that are excellent. Not merely the good but the excellent! Youth face a multitude of temptations. They can and will choose wisely if faithfully taught God's Word in an attractive way and if we surround them with "a hedge of faith and prayer."

A sincere lifestyle that is without offense. Paul describes that lifestyle in these words: "Whether you eat or drink or whatever you do, do all to the glory of God" (1 Cor. 10:31). That takes in everything—the modesty of what a young person wears, what he or she eats, the music listened to, the care of the body, the preservation of sexual purity, one's conversation, traits like honesty and dependability.

As we pray we can do so with full confidence that God's Word can produce youth "without offense"—youth in whose hearts Christ "is effecting transformations so amazing that Satan, with all his triumphant boasting, with all his confederacy of evil united against God and the laws of His government, stands viewing them as a fortress impregnable to his sophistries and delusions" (*Testimonies to Ministers*, 18).

A lifestyle filled with the fruits of righteousness which are by Jesus Christ. We ask for a lot when we make Paul's request in Philippians 1:9 that God give His people a love that abounds more and more! But God is well able to do far more than we can ask or even dream (Eph. 3:20). Let's ask, daily, even hourly. Let's continually send up silent petitions for youth everywhere.

What would happen if . . . ?

In mid-August (1997) I gave a handout about using Philippians 1:9-11 to Julie Hill, a senior nursing student from Pacific Union College.

She had come to Andrews to represent the Pacific Northwest in NET '98 planning sessions with Glenn Aufderhar, Media Center director; Dwight Nelson, NET '98 speaker; and others. I met her when eating lunch at the

AU cafeteria. As we talked, she spoke of being nervous about being on an important committee.

That evening I dropped by the dorm to give her a copy of my *Whatever It Takes Praying* and other materials about prayer. We prayed that she would do well and that she would be a blessing back at PUC, where she would be a resident assistant in the girls' dorm during the 1997-98 school year.

In a note that came in today's mail, she thanked me for the things I had given, and added, "I have memorized Philippians 1:9-11, and have been using it several times a day. Thank you for the suggestion."

Julie came to Berrien Springs again in October 1997, and her enthusiasm for using Paul's Philippians prayer for the girls on her floor at PUC thrilled me. Here's her testimony:

> I started praying for the girls on my hall the first week of August, using Philippians 1:9-11. As the school year began, I went to each girl's room and suggested: "With your studies and adjustments to college life, it will be easy to lose touch with God. Won't you make a commitment *now* to plan some time each day for God?"
>
> As the year continued, I started praying with some of them. Then one of my girls came to me and asked for Bible studies. Soon I had three Bible studies going, with a total of fifteen girls on my hall, three of whom were non-Adventists. Each time they would excitedly pray for a revival on campus.
>
> Then three other resident advisors heard what I was doing, and started Bible studies in their halls. All the revivals in history have started from Bible study and prayer. Revival *is* happening on my hall at PUC.

What might be the results if thousands of us were to unite in using Philippians 1:9-11 as a fervent request for the youth of the entire world? In Matthew 18:19 Christ assured us that the prayers of even two people can make a difference.

At the start of each new day, why not make "still more and more" your highest purpose for that day? The devotional book *Our High Calling* puts it like this: "The soul passion is more, more. This is the real want of the soul. We want more of the divine grace, more enlightenment, more faith" (188).

Possible applications of the content of this chapter include:

- *Continue or begin using Philippians 1:9-11 as you daily pray for Adventist youth and Generation X seekers.*
- *If possible, recruit one or more others to meet with you once a week to pray for God's blessing on NET '98 and every other evangelistic effort between now and into A.D. 2000.*

8

Transformed and Kept

"Blessed be the God and Father of our Lord Jesus Christ,
who according to His abundant mercy has begotten us
again to a living hope, through the resurrection of Jesus Christ from
the dead, to an inheritance incorruptible
and undefiled and that does not fade away, reserved in heaven for you,
who are kept by the power of God through faith to the salvation ready
to be revealed" (1 Peter 1:3-5).

Today is Labor Day, September 1, 1997. As I awoke I recalled that it was fifty years ago this month that I first set foot on an Adventist campus. After taking the *Voice of Prophecy* senior Bible course, I had been baptized in August 1946, as a sixteen-year-old high school junior. I finished my senior year in public school then spent the summer of 1947 doing literature evangelism in my home state of Oklahoma.

I arrived at night to what was then Southwestern Junior College, in Keene, Texas. I'll never forget the thrills, during the days that followed, of getting acquainted with the campus. It was a preview of what exploring the New Jerusalem will be like.

I am the oldest of four children and the first to be baptized. Our mother and father were not pleased when I started keeping the Sabbath. During the first year that I attempted to live as a Seventh-day Adventist, I found much help from a pocket New Testament I had purchased.

I liked to take it to a creek that flowed through our farm, where I knelt on the gravel and talked to God about the above passage from 1 Peter. I especially prayed for God's help in keeping the Sabbath.

Praying for Adventist youth

God brought the same passage to mind as I read my Bible this Labor Day morning. It has become my custom each morning to write a Bible passage for the day on a 3 by 5 card, which I keep with me to use as subject matter for prayer during the day. I did this on Labor Day with 1 Peter 1:3-5.

For an outdoor place to pray, I cycled to a university cornfield. There, hidden in the corn, I could use this passage as I prayed for about fifteen minutes for Adventist children and youth.

Before leaving the house I had checked the 1997 *Yearbook* to find out the number of schools our church operates. Here are the figures, taken from 1995 statistics:

- 81 colleges/universities
- 930 secondary schools
- 4,522 elementary schools
- 913,315 students

I rounded off the number of students to 900,000 and then memorized the figures so I could mention them every day, along with Adventist students in public schools, in my prayers.

Would you consider doing something similar? Round the figures off to 80 colleges, 930 secondary schools, and 4,500 elementary schools, with a total of just over 900,000 students.

Let me say it again: Every sincere prayer, backed with faith in Christ's merits, has an influence for eternity. If you are using Philippians 1:9-11 in prayers for Adventist youth everywhere, every prayer makes a difference—so much so that in eternity you will repeatedly be thrilled as you see how much influence your prayers had on these youth.

Kept by a heavenly garrison

Upon kneeling in the cornfield, I took the 1 Peter 1:3-5 card and in behalf of our youth asked God to give them everything that passage mentions: His abundant mercy, living hope, and a faith that would keep them within God's protective care.

I had checked the *SDA Bible Commentary* and found that the word *kept* comes from a Greek word that means "to garrison"—a military term that has to do with the protection provided by a garrison of troops.

NET '98 is for all ages, though its messages are slanted to Generation X; namely, people between thirteen and thirty-three. In the current membership of ten million in the Seventh-day Adventist Church, probably at least five million are between thirteen and thirty-three. What would happen if tens of thousands of us would begin to incorporate the requests of Philippians

1:9-11 into prayers for ourselves and for the millions of Generation Xers right in our own church?

Let's pray for such a complete transformation that each will become "filled with the fruits of righteousness, which are by Jesus Christ to the glory and praise of God" (Phil.1:11). Let's also pray at the start of each day that God's angels—a heavenly military garrison—will surround each young person all day and all through whatever dangers and temptations the night brings.

Praying for youth everywhere

God's love also takes in the hundreds of millions of children and youth in today's world who come from non-Christian backgrounds, including those in the Moslem and Hindu worlds.

Rhonda, a young woman from Lebanon, enrolled in my Workshop in Prayer class this fall (1997). Her parents objected strongly when they learned that she intended to become a Seventh-day Adventist. Because she left the Greek Orthodox faith most of her family disowned her. Now that she belongs to a Sabbath-keeping church, they look upon her as a Jew and therefore a traitor.

When I asked her how she learned about our church, she replied, "Through the health message." She is taking dietetics at Andrews, and hopes to eventually open a chain of vegetarian restaurants. "I want you to marry a wealthy Arab," her father told her, but she is dating an Adventist young man who is studying for the ministry.

She represents millions of young Arabs who would fall in love with Jesus if only they had opportunity to learn about Him. That brings into sharp focus an awesome prayer need: to regularly ask God to richly bless Adventist World Radio (AWR). Through God's providence AWR now reaches all through the Middle East.

Most of Iran's 67 million people, for example, speak Farsi. When AWR began its Farsi broadcasts in April 1996, letters began coming to the production headquarters in Cyprus within days. By November 1997, AWR was broadcasting messages in more than fifty languages, and keeps adding new ones.

As you continue using Philippians 1:9-11 please pray it in behalf of the third of a billion children and youth in Arab countries.

Building friends where you live

Before feeding the 4,000, Jesus told the disciples, "I have compassion on the multitude . . . . I do not want to send them away hungry" (Matt. 15:32). All through His ministry Christ mingled with people, showed sympathy for them, ministered to their needs, and won their confidence. He then invited them to follow Him.

What might happen if each young believer who reads this would ask God to help him or her to develop a similar approach? What if he or she built a redemptive friendship with someone who doesn't know Christ? Could thousands be added to the attenders of NET '98 and other evangelistic meetings? Could additional hundreds and even thousands be won to Christ?

What do you think? What might you do with the content of this chapter? Consider these suggestions:

- *Ask God to give you a burden to pray for all Adventist youth—those in church schools and those in public schools. Then memorize the statistics about Adventist education given in this chapter to use in your prayers.*
- *In his Philippians 1:9-11 prayer, Paul began, "This I pray, that your love may abound still more and more in knowledge and all discernment, that you may approve the things that are excellent." If you haven't already done so, take the expression "still more and more" and blend it into your every request for spiritual blessings.*
- *If you are memorizing Phil.1:9-11, try to pray it every day and many times a day in behalf of all children and youth, including those in the Moslem world. Ask God to especially bless Adventist World Radio.*

9

Nine Teen Thugs and Two Fourteen-Year-Old Girls

**"His powerful Word is sharp as a surgeon's scalpel,
cutting through everything. . . . Nothing and no one
is impervious to God's Word (Heb. 4:12, 13, The Message paraphrase).**

"We're going to kill you," a hooded teenager sneered as he stepped toward the two girls that he and eight others had surrounded.

The place: a dangerous, dark neighborhood in Venezuela.

The girls: Damaris Briceno and Inez Perz, two fourteen-year-olds selling Adventist books and magazines to earn school tuition.

The situation: At noon that day Inez had gone to a lady's house for a Bible study and found a note on the door asking her to return at 6:00 p. m. Damaris had another appointment, so Inez went alone to the study.

The study lasted longer than expected, but finally Damaris rejoined Inez, and they started home. Before entering a particularly dangerous area, Inez and Damaris stopped to pray again and to claim this promise: "I will never leave you nor forsake you" (Heb. 13:5).

"Do it!"

Suddenly a sense of danger sent a cold chill down their backs. "In the distance we saw something move," Inez said. "Then we saw several men coming toward us. Damaris clutched my hand in terror. Again we stopped and prayed."

When they opened their eyes, they were surrounded by nine teenage boys. "God is with us," Damaris whispered. Then they stood very quiet.

The oldest youth turned to a gang member and said, "Do it!"

The one spoken to held up a knife. "Drop the bag or we'll kill you," he snarled. Inez put her bag on the ground and told the boy, "God loves you." Startled, he just stood there, surprised and confused.

"Get back in line," the leader shouted to the younger boy.

"Damaris and I prayed silently that God would work a miracle to save us," Inez said. "Then I began to talk to them of Jesus' love. I told them that Jesus left His home in heaven to come here to die for them."

"Why are you telling us this?" the leader demanded. "We came to rob you, not for a sermon!"

Inez answered, "Jesus came to save you and to change you from a sinner to one of His followers. And we must tell you about Him."

The leader pulled a gun from his belt and held it to her head. "If you keep talking, I'm going to kill you," he growled.

"Even if you kill me, I must tell you that Jesus loves you and wants to change your life," Inez replied.

"You're crazy," the leader said as he lowered his gun and asked, "How does Jesus change people? What can He do for me?"

"Jesus loves you," Inez continued, "the same as He loved those who crucified Him." The boys seemed surprised that the girls didn't fear for their lives.

"Aren't we going to kill them?"

The leader asked, "How do we change?"

"What's going on?" one youth demanded. "Aren't we going to kill them?"

"I can't kill these girls," the leader answered. "I'm getting a feeling I can't resist."

Inez told him, "You are feeling God's love. He wants to change you."

"God is in this place," Inez said. "Jesus is calling you to follow Him." She had been hugging her Bible and held it out to the leader. Slowly he took it and said, "Thank you very much."

"Don't you remember that we came to kill these girls?" one boy asked.

Inez turned to him and said, "Jesus wants to give you His new life too."

"You're crazy," he spat out as he slapped her across the face. Inez spoke quietly to him, "Jesus loves you, and He will love you no matter what you do."

Damaris then spoke, "God has a purpose for your life."

"I'd like to know what purpose God has for *me*," he said.

"Maybe this will help you to understand," Damaris said as she handed him and each boy a magazine. Then she said, "God bless you. We're going now."

The boys parted and let them walk through the circle. Down the road the girls turned, waved, and said, "Someday we will see you again. The Lord is going to bring us together."

"My Bible!"

The girls continued to sell books and magazines. Five months later the sales director asked them to attend a training seminar at a small church two hours away by bus. After arrival, as they approached the church, they noticed a tall youth staring at them.

Inez smiled and greeted him, "Good afternoon. My name is Inez."

"And my name is Damaris," her companion said.

The young man smiled and said, "I think we have met before."

"Yes," Inez responded. "You look familiar, but I do not know your name."

The young man handed her a Bible and asked, "Do you recognize this?"

"I caught my breath," Inez said. "It was my old Bible—the one I'd given to the gang leader. I stared at him in amazement."

"Do you remember when you gave me this Bible and told me it would change my life? You were right. Jesus has worked a miracle in my life."

The girls listened as José told how he had begun to read that Bible, searching for the peace and love he saw in their lives. After they visited a few minutes, José asked, "Would you like to see the others who were there that night?"

They entered the church and found eight young men sitting near the front on one side. As they talked, they learned that all nine boys had been baptized. They had heard about the seminar and had prayed that the girls would come.

Sixty-one new believers

After the seminar the boys invited Inez and Damaris to visit their homes. Inez asked José, "How was your life before you were converted to Jesus?"

With tears José told the girls that he had felt unloved and worthless. Those feelings had pulled him into a life of crime. "But," he added with a smile, "from the night I met you girls I realized that there was hope for me."

The families of the boys greeted the girls with smiles and hugs. They said that the teenage toughs had returned home that night somehow changed. They no longer spent time terrorizing people. Instead, they spent hours studying the Bible and the magazines the girls had given them. At the time of this writing, five years later, they are leaders in their church and community. Their families, as they saw the changes in them, began to ask questions. Each of the nine young men has led his family, along with friends, to accept Christ and be baptized. By 1995, fifty-two others also had been baptized.

As you seek to apply this story to your life:

- *Compare the Bible statement at the start of this chapter with the experience the chapter relates. What are your conclusions?*
- *Prayerfully ask yourself, "Am I experiencing the power found in God's Word? What changes would it take for me to get really excited about studying it?"*

10

Something New Every Day

"Therefore every scribe instructed concerning the kingdom of heaven is like a householder who brings out of his treasure things new and old" (Matt. 13:52).

Jesus loved to use parables and illustrations. In one message—the Sermon on the Mount—He used more than twenty object lessons or illustrations. The preceding verse was the last of eight parables Jesus told in His Matthew 13 Sermon by the Sea. See if you agree with the following interpretation:

- The householder would be the believer.
- The treasure is God's Word.
- Things new would be new facts, new information, new insights that one discovers in prayerfully studying the Bible.
- Things old would be information—facts, truths, etc.—already known and that you can freely share.

When as a teenager I started taking the Voice of Prophecy Bible course, I found something new all the time, and I still find verses or ideas that are new to me. This is especially true when I read from a version or paraphrase I haven't used before.

In my Workshop in Prayer classes, students purchase a devotional book from which they read daily. For about fifteen years we used *My Life Today.* A sentence I always emphasized was this: "Every day you should learn something new from the Scriptures" (22).

The author goes on to suggest that if we would pray for wisdom and understanding, we would continually "find new glories in the Word of God" (ibid.).

I find that happening all the time. For memory's sake, I record the new insights under SN (Something New) in a journal.

Let me share an example:

Scarred hands lifted in an oath

One day last week I focused on a chapter I use frequently when praying for children and youth; namely, Isaiah 49. I cherish Isaiah 49 as "subject matter for prayer" for two reasons.

- In verse 16 Christ says, "See, I have inscribed you on the palms of My hands." In praying for specific people, I like to visualize their name next to a scar on Christ's hand. Sometimes I do the same for an entire group or for a whole nation.
- The end of Isaiah 49 provides the second reason. Verse 24 asks, "Shall the prey be taken from the mighty?" Or as the NASB words it, "from the tyrant" In verse 25 God answers: "Even the captives of the mighty shall be taken away, and the prey of the terrible be delivered, for I will contend with him who contends with you, and I will save your children."

The tyrant obviously is Satan. And his prey? Children and others who have abandoned Christ. Verse 25 has brought hope to uncounted numbers of parents whose hearts have been broken by prodigal sons and daughters.

My "something new" came from verses 22 and 23, which begins, "Thus says the Lord, 'Behold, I will lift my hand in an oath to the nations, and set up My standard for the peoples; they shall bring your sons in their arms, and your daughters shall be carried on their shoulders."

I see this, like other passages in Isaiah, as a promise of many children and youth won to the church, including from Moslem lands (see Isa. 44:1-5; 54:1-3). But only last week did I connect "Behold, I will lift My hands in an oath to the nations" with the "I have inscribed you on the palms of My hands" of verse 16. *That helped me see those uplifted hands as nail-scarred hands.*

Do you see what that means? Christ's nail-scarred hands are uplifted as He takes an oath to the nations that children from every land will be won to Himself.

Revelation 14 mandates that the gospel *will* go to "every nation, tribe, tongue, and people." The God who died on the cross lifts up wounded hands to declare that *it will happen.* We can pray with courage.

An insight about ministry

Did you know that Scripture calls prayer a ministry? Here's what Paul said about a friend who helped start a church at Colosse: "Epaphras, who is one of you, a servant of Christ, greets you, always laboring fervently for you in prayers, that you may stand perfect and complete in all the will of God" (Col. 4:12).

Always laboring fervently for you in prayers. As I copied the above verse on a 3 by 5 card to keep with me during the day, I included this next verse: "For I bear him witness that he has a great zeal for you, and those who are in Laodicea, and those in Hierapolis." The marginal reading for *zeal* is *concern*. That alternate reading and the mention of Laodicea became my "something new" that morning.

God's message to modern Laodicea in Revelation 3:14-22 calls for concern about our lukewarmness. As a comment on the importance of prayer as a ministry, consider this:

> The greatest victories gained for the cause of God are not the result of labored argument, ample facilities, wide influence or abundance of means; they are gained in the audience chamber with God, when with earnest, agonizing faith men lay hold upon the mighty arm of power (*Gospel Workers*, 259).

I see this as applying on the family level as well as for denominational needs. If you have children who are lukewarm, or who have left Christ, you might want to write Isaiah 49:16, 24, 25 on a 3 by 5 card just for your own encouragement.

Perhaps you could even keep it with you, and whenever you have a spare moment, present it to God as you pray for the indifferent ones. Here's one of my "something new" discoveries from this morning: I read from *In Heavenly Places* that humble believers will see that "their persevering prayers will bring souls to the cross. Heavenly angels will respond to their self-sacrificing efforts" (68). That told me perseverance can make a world of difference.

Here are two more suggestion for this chapter's content:

- *Begin your own "something new" plan.*
- *If you possess volume 5 of Testimonies for the Church or can borrow one from the church library, read on pages 322 and 323 how God answered the prayers of a mother who "laid her finger upon the texts, presenting before God His own words, and pleaded as only a mother can."*

11

More "Something New" Discoveries

**Believe in the Lord your God, and you shall be established;
believe His prophets, and you shall prosper (2 Chron. 20:20).**

In the early 1980s, as I rewrote the academy grade eleven Bible text titled *Anchored*, the steering committee agreed we should include a lesson that we called "Something New Every Day." In it we listed and illustrated nine different methods students could use to find new ideas and insights as they studied their Bibles.

These methods were: (1) look for stories new to you, (2) look for verses new to you, (3) examine the context, (4) use marginal cross references, (5) check marginal alternate readings, (6) look at other versions, (7) search for new insights in an already familiar passage, (8) look for new insights in Spirit of Prophecy comments, and (9) read what others have discovered.

For myself the richest source for new insights has been the writings of Ellen White. In the Workshop in Prayer syllabus that I used until my *Whatever It Takes Praying* was published, I had a section of thirty-six pages titled "Selected Promises." Each page had two columns. On the left we had typed out the 160 Bible promises, followed with the 50 command-promises. Then on the right we had an Ellen White statement with each that often provided a new insight.

Promises and commands

The first Bible statement we underline is the promise of a Saviour in Genesis 3:15. There God told Lucifer, "I will put enmity between you and the woman, and between your seed and her Seed." Ellen White takes "I will put enmity" and comments: "This enmity is not naturally entertained. . . . It is the grace that Christ implants in the soul which creates in man enmity against Satan" (*The Great Controversy*, 505, 506).

The first promise in the New Testament, like the first in the Old, deals with sin: "Call His name Jesus, for He will save His people from their sins" (Matt. 1:21). As a comment, I found this: "No sooner is the name of Jesus mentioned in love and tenderness than angels of God draw near, to soften and subdue the heart" (*Colporteur Ministry*, 112).

Students underline this promise from Luke: "For with God nothing will be impossible" (1:37). The comment I found seems especially for NET '98 and all media evangelism: "The message will go with power . . . to all nations, tongues, and peoples. . . . It will grow to large proportions. . . . God will work with great power if you will walk in all humility of mind before Him" (*Life Sketches*, 209).

As I thought about "grow to large proportions" I prayed especially for India. An article in the September 8, 1997, issue of the South Bend *Tribune* about Mother Teresa's death reported that only an estimated 2 percent of India's 970 million people are Christians. We need to pray that God will abundantly bless NET '98 as Pastor Nelson's messages are downlinked in that country, where most people are either Hindus or Moslems.

One-third of earth's nearly six billion people live in two countries, India and China. Let's enter into heart-searching and prayer and ask God to expand His work in those two countries to "large proportions."

And speaking of heart-searching and repentance, here's a command of Paul's that students underline: "I desire that in every place the men should pray, lifting holy hands without anger or quarreling: also that women should adorn themselves modestly and sensibly in seemly [NEB: becoming] apparel, not with braided hair [NEB: elaborate hair-styles] or gold or pearls or costly array, but by good deeds" (1 Tim. 2:8-10, RSV).

For a comment I found this: "Here the Lord, through His apostle, speaks expressly against the wearing of gold. . . . That ring encircling your finger may be very plain, but it is useless, and the wearing of it has a wrong influence upon others" (*Testimonies*, 4:630).

A personal experience

When at sixteen I was studying the *Voice of Prophecy* Bible lessons, one month the Bible school sent *The Impending Conflict*—a booklet that contains the closing ten chapters of *The Great Controversy*. An aunt and cousin, good Baptist people, had noted my developing interest in religion and had invited me to go with them to an Easter pageant near Lawton, Oklahoma.

The Impending Conflict had just arrived, and I had found it so gripping that I could hardly put it down. On the way to Lawton I sat in the back seat reading it much of the way. My aunt threatened to take it away from me. I put it aside but not for long. The deep impression it made led me to tell myself, "I've got to join the Seventh-day Adventist Church."

At another time the *Voice of Prophecy* sent *Behold the Man*, by Taylor Bunch, as the booklet of the month. It contained many quotations from *The Desire of Ages*. As I read the quotations I told myself, "I've got to find a copy of that book."

A suitcase of books

I had started attending the little Adventist church at Ponca City, Oklahoma, and one Sabbath a family there invited me to go with them to camp meeting at Oklahoma City. Elder H. M. S. Richards, Sr. was there, and I made a decision to be baptized. I also spent a lot of time in the book tent, where I purchased *The Desire of Ages, The Great Controversy*, and other Ellen White books. I about filled my small suitcase with books.

I knew my parents would not approve of my book purchases. When I got home I slipped them under my bed for a time. They didn't stay there. I simply cannot put into words how much I appreciate the way Ellen White's books glorify Christ and exalt the Bible and its truths.

To close this chapter, let me suggest:

• *If you have a copy of* The Great Controversy *handy, for a special thrill read the chapter titled "God's People Delivered."*
• *Several years ago Pastor Dwight, the NET '98 speaker, remarked that he had read* The Desire of Ages *seven times and had done underlining with a different colored pencil each time. Even if you have already read it, you might want to do so again. As you do, I can promise you one thing: With every chapter you'll find more and more reasons to love Jesus. For me the most gripping chapter in the book has been the one titled "Calvary." One could spend an entire week or even a month reflecting on the pen pictures of Jesus found in that chapter.*

12

Seven Promises That Cover Every Need

**My God shall supply all your need according
to His riches in glory by Christ Jesus (Phil. 4:19).**

In chapter 8 I mentioned that it had been fifty years ago, in the fall of 1947, that I had first set foot on an Adventist campus. I had been baptized the previous summer and had worked as a literature evangelist before going to Southwestern Junior College.

While doing colporteur work I had developed a constant thirst. Shortly after a physical, the campus doctor called me in and gently told me "You have diabetes."

It was the juvenile kind, which doesn't respond to pills like adult-onset diabetes sometimes does, so I started taking insulin. I have never needed large doses and have never had a coma from blood sugar being too high. On the other hand, I sometimes let my blood sugar get too low, which can cause unconsciousness.

God gave me a wife who has wonderfully watched out for me, and as I look back, I recognize that being a diabetic has brought many blessings. I eat more carefully and have a strong motivation to get exercise. We praise God for always providing for our medical and physical needs.

Wondrous spiritual blessings

Spiritually, God has also met every need. I shall be forever grateful for the Bible and its truths and for God leading me to these treasures through the Voice of Prophecy. Now that I generally record my "something new" discoveries I have been doubly blessed. On most days I write these new insights in a journal.

I also love the Spirit of Prophecy books. My wife and I have almost all the 100 plus books and compilations now in print. As mentioned earlier, I try to write a Scripture passage during my morning study time on a 3 by 5 card for prayer use at later times during the day. The other morning I jotted down a Bible passage and then included this from *In Heavenly Places:* "Every sincere prayer that is offered is mingled with the efficacy of Christ's blood. If the answer is deferred, it is because God desires us to show holy boldness in claiming the pledged word of God" (74).

What prayer boldness that inspires! When I pray, collectively, for our eighty-one Adventist colleges and 930 academies and the more than 4,500 elementary schools and for all youth in public schools, I can do so boldly. I try to do that every day, and many times a day, and in doing so I pray with a thankful awareness that my petition "is mingled with the efficacy of Christ's blood"!

Seven promises from Genesis

In my Workshop in Prayer class we start our Bible underlining with seven promises from Genesis. I tell my students, "In these seven promises God has provided for just about every need you could ever have." As I explain why, see if you agree.

The first is Genesis 3:15, in which God told Lucifer that a Seed of the woman would bring redemption and in doing so would inflict a fatal wound upon him. God also said this: "I will put enmity, Lucifer, between you and the woman."

Almost every morning God brings that promise to mind as I pray. I take it and plead, "Help me, today, to hate sin." I often ask the same blessing for those on my prayer list and for all the youth of our church.

We next underline the promise in Genesis 8:22 in which God promises there will be a seedtime and harvest while the earth lasts. I see Genesis 8:22 as a promise for our physical needs: food, clothing, and other things that earth's harvests produce.

In the third promise, Genesis 12:2, God told Abraham, "I will bless you . . . and make you a blessing." I see that as a promise for every child of God. I also mention it almost every morning, and then in my journaling I generally record how God either has blessed or has made me a blessing. It's a good way to get an answered prayer every day.

We then underline another promise to Abraham that is for every believer: "Do not be afraid, Abram, I am your shield, your exceedingly great reward" (Gen. 15:1). He's our shield for protection, and in His friendship He is our *exceedingly great reward.*

The fifth promise is another one to Abraham, "I will make you exceedingly fruitful" (Genesis 17:6, first part). The context shows it to be a promise of many descendants. I compare that with John 15:7, 8, where Jesus said: "If you abide in

Me, and My words abide in you, you will ask what you desire, and it shall be done for you. By this is My Father glorified that you bear much fruit." The fruit in John 15 is not literal descendants but people won to Christ.

The sixth promise I take from Genesis 24, where Abraham sent Eliezer to the city of Nahor to search for a wife for Isaac. Through Abraham, God gave this promise, "He will send His angel before you, and you shall take a wife for my son from there" (Gen. 24:7). I suggest to students, "If marriage is part of God's plan for your life, you can claim this promise as you seek a life partner."

The final promise we underline comes from what God told Jacob when he saw a ladder upon which angels were ascending and descending. "I am with you and will keep you wherever you go," God promised (Gen. 28:15).

Provision for every need

Consider the completeness of what God offers just in His Genesis promises:

- Genesis 3:15—first promise of a Saviour, with this assurance from God, "I will help you to hate sin."
- Genesis 8:22—"While the earth remains, seedtime and harvest . . . shall not cease."
- Genesis 12:2—"I will bless you . . . and you shall be a blessing."
- Genesis 15:1—"I am your shield, your exceedingly great reward."
- Genesis 17:6—"I will make you exceedingly fruitful."
- Genesis 24:40—I will give angel guidance when you are seeking a life partner.
- Genesis 28:15—"I am with you and will keep you wherever you go."

After we discuss these promises, I ask students, "Can you think of any need you have, physically, spiritually, or socially, that wouldn't be covered?" And these are promises from just the first book of the Bible!

In the last half of Hebrews 6, Paul makes a striking statement about God's promise to Abraham in Genesis 12:2 that He will bless him and make him a blessing. Paul points out that God backs this promise by an oath in which "He swore by Himself, saying, 'Surely blessing I will bless you, and multiplying I will multiply you' " (13, 14). I love this wording of Hebrews 6:14 in Peterson's The Message: "I promise that I'll bless you with everything I have—bless and bless and bless!"

Could I suggest a couple of ways you might begin to test Genesis 3:15, 12:2, and the other Genesis promises?

- *You may not see the results until eternity, but on a daily basis pray that right in your own church and community God will be working to develop a hatred of sin in the life of every believer and every seeker.*

• *Each morning for the next week ask God to fulfill Genesis 12:2 for you by making you a special blessing to at least one person that day. At the end of the day review how God answered that prayer. For that week you might want to write two or three sentences each evening about how God answered your request.*

13

A Spirit of Intercession

"I will pour out My Spirit on all flesh; Your sons and daughters . . . Your old men . . . Your young men . . . My menservants . . . My maidservants . . . that whoever calls on the name of the Lord shall be saved" (Joel 2:28, 29, 32).

One thing God has been using to bring an end-time fulfillment of the preceding prophecy has been prayer and ministry conferences. "The first prayer conference I went to," said one academy student, "was at the church in Paradise, California, in April 1995. About thirty youth from Paradise Academy took part. I believe that everyone who participated was changed."

The first session among Adventists called a prayer conference took place in Oregon in 1988. There were seven by 1994, thirteen in 1995, sixty-five in 1996, and eighty-five in 1997. As the numbers increased, the movement needed leadership, and in 1995 Ruthie Jacobsen was asked to direct such conferences in North America.

Chapter 5 mentioned that in the spring of 1995 Ruthie Jacobsen and some youth pastors took ninety American teens to conduct prayer and ministry conferences in England. The leaders spent the first week training the teens. Then these youth spread out through South England to help conduct prayer and ministry conferences—a ministry that blessed both schools and churches and that converted or reconverted the American teens.

"England was extra special to me," said one young woman, "because I had the opportunity to train five other youth in Bible study, prayer, ministry, and in leading groups.

"God taught me the joy of growth and of watching others grow," she added. "It was so exciting to see those I had shared with . . . now so openly and strongly sharing their faith and leading others to Christ. That's really what prayer conferences are for—bringing others to Christ."

Prayer conferences and small groups

I attended my first prayer conference in June 1996, at Dakota Academy. The following October I observed a prayer and ministry conference at Mt. Vernon Academy, and in January 1997 I helped organize a group of thirteen Andrews students who conducted a conference at Broadview Academy. No words are adequate to describe the wonders of what God did at these conferences.

This chapter will be longer than most, and at the close I want to make this suggestion: If every church district in North America could have a prayer and ministry conference during the next two years, I believe that we would see tens or even hundreds of thousands transformed and enriched lives.

At such conferences participants are organized into small groups of eight or ten. Generally, a trained youth facilitator leads the group in Bible study and prayer and in a community ministry. At the final session, usually a Saturday night, all the groups meet together for testimonies and prayer.

Before the final meeting, the groups have spent Sabbath afternoon in community ministries—going door to door offering to pray with people and then leaving *Steps to Christ* or other literature, visiting care homes and hospitals, and taking prayer walks. On a "prayer walk" a group simply walks down a street, prays for the homes and businesses on that street, and when appropriate visits with people working in their yards or out walking.

At the evening meeting people share testimonies about their afternoon experiences and then gather for a final prayer time. In every case something has happened at the last session that I had not seen before among academy youth: a closing prayer time that has almost always lasted at least an hour. Conversions or reconversions almost always take place.

Something similar generally has happened when participants have been mostly adults. Hearts have been broken, tears shed, and earnest prayers offered.

Conducting a conference

While adults help organize events, in most prayer conferences the youth themselves direct most of the activities. The first session at all conferences is a general one at which the youth lead out with singing, prayer, and testimonies.

Those present are then divided into groups of eight or ten, with each group led by a youth facilitator. It's been helpful to divide into groups by a method that ensures a good intermingling. One method: if participants are seated in rows, a leader can have people number off one to five or one to eight or whatever is needed. Then all the ones become the first group, all the twos the second group, etc.

After the small groups have been formed, the facilitators use an icebreaker of some kind that helps participants get acquainted and become relaxed. Here's a sample of possible ice-breaking questions:

- What has been the most unusual (scary, enjoyable, humorous) thing that you have experienced during the last thirty days?
- Have you had a recent answer to prayer that you would be willing to share?

Using the acronym PART

In small group prayer sessions it's best to be seated in a circle. At prayer time participants are encouraged to sit comfortably on the floor or bow where seated. Even in a small group the prayer time may last too long to comfortably kneel.

Both in the small groups and in the general prayer sessions, all are encouraged to pray sentence prayers, using an acronym such as PART (praise, admit, requests, thanksgiving).

The one in charge says something like this: "Our prayer time will use the acronym PART, which stands for praise, admit, requests, and thanksgiving. I will begin with a sentence of *praise and adoration*; then anyone else who wants to say a sentence of praise does so. Instead of going around a circle, let the praise sentences be spontaneous from any part of the circle.

"I will then switch to *admit (confession)*. On this, please avoid things not appropriate to mention out loud and stick to sins like impatience, selfishness, getting irritated, attempting to do too much, neglecting prayer, etc.

"I will next lead into *requests*. During requests, bring only one at a time but feel free to pray more than once. If you wish, open your Bible and include a promise as part of your request.

"We will then close with *thanksgiving*, still using sentence prayers from any part of the circle. At any point during the PART praying, it is appropriate for someone to begin a chorus or read a verse of Scripture."

In the final meeting, all groups meet together and follow the above PART sequence. Breaking into a chorus or hymn during the various parts can bring a powerful sense of the Holy Spirit's presence.

Another pattern sometimes used is ACTS (adoration, confession, thanksgiving, and supplication).

Twice during last school year—once in Grand Rapids, Michigan, at the Wyoming church and at the Worthington Church in Columbus, Ohio, the youth of the church were away, and our students from Andrews had only adults for the conference. Three youth led out, with groups of twenty to thirty persons each. During the final session, where all participants met as a single group, tears would steal down the cheeks of some of us—especially as everyone would join in a chorus or hymn or pray for a prodigal son or daughter.

Bible study in small groups

Bible study in small groups has a life-changing influence. It happens like this:

The eight or ten participants form a circle, and after a prayer they take turns reading the passage selected. The facilitator then has people go through the passage a second time. Each person reads a verse and comments upon it. For each verse, the leader seeks input from other group members. Each is encouraged to ask one or more of these six *observation* questions: "What? Who? Where? When? Why? How?"

Other questions that can be asked about a verse or passage include:

- Is there an *example* for me to follow?
- Is there a *sin* for me to avoid?
- Is there a *command* for me to obey?
- Is there a *promise* for me to claim?
- What is a *truth* in this passage that I can use?

To close the study, the facilitator summarizes two or three usable ideas found in the passage. One Andrews student leader put it this way, "If I don't find something usable in a passage it doesn't mean anything to me."

This evening (September 10, 1997) I slipped into a midweek service of students from Andrews Academy and found fifty young people present. After a half hour for singing and sharing, they split into student-led Bible study groups.

To close, all assembled into one group to pray. One young man prayed intensely about the nearness of Christ's return, and when he ended his prayer there were a lot of "Amens." In another prayer, a young woman thanked God for being a Father to us and then pleaded for Him to give much of the Holy Spirit. As the students prayed, I had a strong awareness of God's presence.

Why ministry is also important

Probably every Adventist college and academy, and a lot of churches, have had weeks of prayer that brought a revival that didn't last. Can that be changed, and if so, how? Some of the early leaders in the prayer conference movement suggest that the answer is in the chapter in *Steps to Christ* entitled

"The Work and the Life."

The three chapters that precede it are titled "Faith and Acceptance," "The Test of Discipleship," and "Growth in Grace." These are about depending on faith rather than feeling after you accept Christ, obeying Him, and growing through abiding in Him. Then "The Work and the Life" talks about the need for ministry. Note what God will do for those who seek to win others to Christ:

> If you will go to work as Christ designs that His disciples shall, and win souls for Him, you will feel the need of a deeper experience and a greater knowledge in divine things, and will hunger and thirst after righteousness. You will plead with God, and your faith will be strengthened, and your soul will drink deeper drafts of the well of salvation. Encountering opposition and trials will drive you to the Bible and prayer. You will grow in grace and the knowledge of Christ, and will develop a rich experience (*Steps to Christ*, 80).

How many benefits do you find in the above paragraph? A suggestion: before reading further, underline each benefit. And if you go to *Steps to Christ* for the paragraph immediately after the one quoted, you'll find nearly a dozen more benefits that come from doing ministry.

God led two youth pastors of my acquaintance, Gary Burns at Andrews Academy and Gary Parks at Paradise Academy in California, to this statement at about the same time. Gary Burns, now chaplain at Dakota Academy, took several of his youth to the prayer conference in England. These young men and women came back transformed youth, and through God's blessing upon them many in Dakota Academy are involved in ministry.

Gary Parks, youth pastor at Paradise Academy, said he had been trying to keep his youth in the church with "spiritual entertainment"—outstanding speakers, musical groups, etc. He got so discouraged he was ready to drop out of the ministry.

Then some of his youth started a Bible study and prayer group. About the same time, Pastor Parks discovered the two paragraphs on page 80 of *Steps to Christ* and asked God to help him train his youth for ministry. He took nearly fifty of his youth to the England conference, and as God has worked through them the Holy Spirit has transformed Paradise Academy into a spiritual powerhouse where youth are continually helping conduct prayer conferences.

When a grandson and I visited a prayer and ministry conference at the Paradise church in May 1997, I ended up in a group led by a ninth-grader. Susan had eight adults in her group, including a physician. She led the Bible study and prayer time so skillfully that I thought to myself, "This young woman has been well-trained and richly blessed by the Holy Spirit!"

Miracles through small groups

Jesus used the small group plan—he took twelve men and used them to launch the Christian church. The numerous house churches of the New Testament began with a small group praying and working together. And in a seven-page message in volume 7 of the *Testimonies* Ellen White writes:

> The formation of small companies as a basis of Christian effort has been presented to me by One who cannot err. If there is a large number in the church, let the members be formed into small companies, to work not only for the church members, but for unbelievers. If in one place there are only two or three who know the truth, let them form themselves into a band of workers (21, 22).

Then in comments applicable to both the large church and the two- or three-member group, Ellen White suggests:

> "Let them keep their bond of union unbroken, pressing together in love and unity, encouraging one another to advance, each gaining courage and strength from the assistance of the others.
>
> "Let them reveal Christlike forbearance and patience, speaking no hasty words, using the talent of speech to build one another up in the most holy faith. Let them labor in Christlike love for those outside the fold, forgetting self in their endeavor to help others. *As they work and pray in Christ's name, their numbers will increase*" (*Testimonies for the Church*, 7:22, emphasis supplied).

I want to close with two bold suggestions:

For the next three church board meetings, put aside everything that you can. To prepare for the first session, photocopy the message titled "Work for Church Members" in *Testimonies for the Church,* volume 7, so that board members can read it in advance. Then discuss how to use the content in your congregation. For the group prayer portion of your session, try the PART method.

For the second board meeting, read and discuss the volume 6 message entitled "The Home Missionary Work," with special attention to the sections titled "Arouse the Idlers" and "The Youth to Be Missionaries."

For the third session, read from volume 7 the messages "Workers From the Ranks" and "Extending the Triumphs of the Cross." And if four such sessions are possible, for the fourth discuss the volume 8 message "The Power Promised."

Here's another bold suggestion. *I have tried to give enough information that you as a church member could organize a small group to test the PART prayer method or the Bible study method, or both, in your own home.* With each option be sure to include prayers for NET '98 and for all evangelism into the year 2000. Here are possible steps you could take:

- *Invite six to eight people to your home for a Bible study and prayer time similar to what this chapter summarizes.*
- *After you have gained some experience leading out, talk to your pastor about having a weekend Prayer and Ministry Conference. Your local conference may have a prayer conference coordinator who could help.*
- *If you do get an OK to have a prayer and ministry conference, let Ruthie Jacobsen, the North American prayer conference coordinator, know what you have in mind. You can write to her at the General Conference, 12501 Old Columbia Pike, Silver Spring, MD 20904.*

14

Praying With Intensity

"Confess your trespasses to one another, and pray for one another, that you may be healed. The effective, fervent prayer of a righteous man avails much" (James 5:16).

Consider questions we might ask about the preceding invitation and promise:

- Does James have in mind healing from physical afflictions, or from spiritual ills, or both?
- Does being intense make one's prayers more effective?
- When you intercede for others, does the length of time you spend in prayer make a difference?
- What about that word *righteous*? What does it take to become righteous enough to expect God to answer?

For the first question, let me share a recent "something new." I used to think James mostly had in mind physical ills. Then a former student who stopped several weeks ago to visit and pray told me of a series of messages he had just given. He pointed out that James's main concern in his book is doubt, double-mindedness, and saying without doing (James 1:5-8; 1:22-24; 2:14-17).

"I concluded," he said, "that while this verse does encourage us to pray for physical ills, the big thing James had in mind was healing from doubt and double-mindedness."

What about the fervency James mentions? Does intercession for others need to be intense to get answers?

Webster defines *intercession* as "prayer, petition, or entreaty in favor of another." The word *intense*, in a positive sense, means "earnest, fervent, firm purpose, great seriousness."

Ordinarily prayer should not be an experience in agony. Getting "worked up" resembles the prayers of the priests of Baal on Mount Carmel, who shouted and even cut themselves (1 Kings 18:28).

In contrast, Elijah's prayer must have taken less than a minute (see 1 Kings 18:36, 37). His petition, though brief, was decidedly fervent. He *knew* God was listening.

Adequate time for prayer

How long does one need to press God for an answer?

No one "earns credit" by the length of time he or she prays. As a monk Martin Luther sometimes tried to pray all night. He then felt condemned when he would fall asleep.

It does, however, take time to pray effectively. Months ago God convicted me that if I would spend at least thirty minutes each morning in actual prayer, I would accomplish more for the advancement of His kingdom than by everything else I might get done during that entire day. To help keep thirty minutes from getting crowded out, I am working on these habits:

- Each morning I ask God to lead me to a Scripture passage as subject matter for that day's prayers, which I write on a 3 by 5 card. I talk to God about that passage during my private prayer, but I also keep it with me for use as I come and go during the day.
- I have a notebook I have labeled "Prayer Log" in which I record the approximate time spent interceding for others during the previous day.
- I generally don't spend all or even a major part of the thirty minutes on my knees. I have memorized enough Bible prayers that I can, if alone, combine some of my prayer time with a morning walk. I also sometimes pray aloud while riding a bicycle.

It will take time, but I'd like to recommend that you select several Bible prayers, especially from Paul and the Psalms, to commit to memory. As you use Philippians 1:9-11 and others, rewording and expanding the key ideas, you will find it much easier to spend up to a half hour or longer in fervent prayer.

That word *righteous*

The suggestion that "the prayers of a *righteous* man avails much" used to trouble me. I certainly didn't *feel* righteous.

Do you have a similar problem? I got a lot of help from the repeated references in John 14–16 to praying *in Christ's name* (John 14:13, 14; 15:16; 16:23, 24, 26). Here's a summary of what that involves:

> In Christ's name His followers are to stand before God. Through the value of the sacrifice made for them, they are of value in the Lord's sight. Because of the imputed righteousness of Christ they are accounted precious. For Christ's sake the Lord pardons those that fear Him. He does not see in them the vileness of the sinner. He recognizes in them the likeness of His Son, in whom they believe (*The Desire of Ages*, 667).

When you rely on Jesus, His character stands in place of your character, and that is why your fervent prayer "avails much." Now compare that fact with one more suggestion:

> We must not only pray in Christ's name, but by the inspiration of the Holy Spirit. . . . When with earnestness and intensity we breathe a prayer in the name of Christ, there is in that very intensity a pledge from God that He is about to answer our prayer "exceeding abundantly above all that we ask or think." Eph. 3:20 (*Christ's Object Lessons*, 147).

A how-to suggestion

The idea of actually talking to God for a full thirty minutes or more may seem impossible to you, but I have discovered a method that helps. That's the practice I mentioned in chapter 2: including parts or all of specific Bible prayers.

I have listed the names of about fifty youth in my prayer log. As I pray collectively for these youth, I often begin with this passage from Psalm 90:

> Let Your work appear to Your servants, and your glory to their children. And let the beauty of the Lord our God be upon us, and establish the work of our hands for us; yes, establish the work of our hands (Ps. 90:16, 17).

What am I asking God to do? I interpret it like this:

Let Your work appear to Your servants. I see God's works as including His wonders in nature, the Scriptures, and His work in changing human hearts. The more I see young lives being changed the more I plead, "More and more, Lord. Do it more and more *and still more!* "

And your glory to Your children. Of Christ John wrote, "We beheld His glory," and then added, "full of grace and truth" (John 1:14). This suggests that Christ's glory is His character, His personality, one full of grace and truth. Thus when I ask God to reveal His glory to my children and students, I am asking two things: (1) that my own example before them will reflect the character of Christ, and (2) that God will do "whatever it takes" to reveal Himself to them.

And let the beauty of the Lord our God be upon us. Again, I am asking this both for myself and for all youth. In praying it I often include this statement from Psalm 34: "They looked to Him and were radiant, and their faces were not ashamed" (5).

Every year at Andrews University, I get acquainted with scores of students whose faces reflect the radiance of Christ. I love praying for them, and for all of what is probably three to four million Adventist children and youth in our world church. As I pray, "Let the beauty of the Lord our God be upon them," I find it easy to be intense.

And establish the work of our hands for us; yes, establish the work of our hands. Note the "*establish . . . for us.*" Jesus told the disciples and us, "Without Me you can do nothing" (John 15:5).

Children and youth will never be transformed by our wisdom or skill or eloquence. As we share His Word with them, God *must work powerfully by His Spirit.* I can and should do my best, but I must depend totally upon God's Word and upon His Spirit.

The book *100 Heart Reaching Illustrations* relates that a Dr. A. C. Dixon once said that when we rely upon organization, we get what organization can do. If we rely on education, we get what education can do. If we rely on eloquence we get what eloquence can do. "But," he added, "when we rely upon prayer we get what God can do" (Theodore W. Engstrom, compiler, *100 Heart Reaching Illustrations* (Grand Rapids, Mich.: Zondervan, 1949), 73).

That sense of total dependence on God may be our greatest need. More and more I am also expressing dependence on the blood of Christ as I pray. The above book mentions that one time Napoleon called his officers together, spread out a large map, pointed his finger to a certain spot where he had put a red dot, and said, "Gentlemen, if it were not for that red spot, I could conquer the world."

That red spot was the British Isles. *Testimonies to Ministers* indicates that from time to time Satan calls some of his angels together for a counsel meeting (472). Could it be that at times he points to a hill near Jerusalem and says, "If it were not for a place called Calvary, I could conquer the universe"?

Let's keep depending on Christ's blood as we pray!

- *Consider again the last two verses of the book of James. Does that passage help confirm the idea that the prayer for the sick includes those who are lukewarm and/or double-minded?*

- *Think and pray about the last section of this chapter. If you are ready for a second prayer to use when interceding for youthful friends, write Psalm 90:16, 17 on a 3 by 5 card and use the card as needed in praying for them.*

15

Prayer As a Science

"Lord, teach us to pray" (Luke 11:1).
"Lord, increase our faith" (Luke 17:5).

Imagine yourself taking a tour of a place in heaven called "God's treasury." You might find a department named "Delayed blessings"—a place where God keeps things prayed for until the right time to send them. In Heaven's accounting department you'd also find a record of requests to which God said No.

"God has not always answered my prayers," Mrs. Billy Graham told an audience of women. "If He had, I would have married the wrong man—several times."

Prayer has been called a school—"the school of prayer." To enroll, one asks, as did the disciples, "Lord, teach me to pray."

A chapter in the book *Education* titled "Faith and Prayer" helped influence me to start the class at Andrews University called "Workshop in Prayer." There the author suggests: "Prayer and faith are closely allied, and they need to be studied together. In the prayer of faith there is a divine science; it is a science that everyone who would make his lifework a success must understand" (257).

That got my attention! There's a "divine science" in the prayer of faith—and *it's a science that everyone who would make his lifework a success must understand!* The study of faith and prayer is for every person who wants to succeed in life.

Why is prayer called a "science"? Isn't it because, like in chemistry, it's governed by laws? Through understanding and praying in harmony with those laws, or conditions, our answers to prayer markedly increase.

Surveying the conditions

A chapter called "The Privilege of Prayer," in *Steps to Christ*, contains this summary of conditions for answered prayer: feel our need (Isa. 44:3), not cherish sin (Ps. 66:18), faith (Heb. 11:6), a forgiving spirit (Matt. 6:12), perseverance (Col.4:2), asking that God's will be done (Matt. 26:39), and praying in Christ's name (John 14:13).

The Bible also mentions specific sins that can restrict the flow of God's blessing. Robbing God in tithes and offerings is a common one (Mal. 3:8-11). Another is tensions between a husband and wife (1 Peter 3:7). Still another is not hearing the cry of the poor (Prov. 31:13). Indulgence of appetite also restricts what God can do for us and can bring on physical ills.

It's interesting to note that indulgence of appetite, along with a desire for a higher status, was behind Eve's sin. In Genesis 3, the story of the Fall, you'll find the word *eat* or its derivatives thirteen times.

Pride and self-importance also restrict what God can do for individuals. Pride, as the Laodicean message of Revelation 3:14-21 points out, can cause an individual or a group to be as repulsive as lukewarm 7UP. Proverbs 6:16-19 puts pride at the top of the list of seven things that God hates.

Removing the hindrances

Just about every sin and hindrance I've listed can be traced to unbelief. David testified of God's Old Testament people, "They . . . limited the Holy One of Israel" (Ps. 78:41). And how did they do this? The context twice says they "did not believe" (Ps. 78:22, 32).

The first step in getting rid of unbelief, and of the sins that hinder us from getting answers to prayer, is to fasten our eyes upon Jesus. In the opening verses of Hebrews 12, after an entire chapter about faith, Paul urges us to "lay aside every weight, and the sin which so easily ensnares us" (Heb. 12:1). That weight, the context makes clear, is unbelief.

Here's the solution Paul suggests: "Let us run with endurance the race that is set before us, looking unto Jesus, the author and finisher of our faith, who for the joy that was set before Him endured the cross, despising the shame, and has set down at the right hand of the throne of God" (Heb. 12:1, 2).

The key phrase is *looking to Jesus*. The Today's English Version puts the first part of verse 2: "Let us keep our eyes fixed on Jesus, on whom our faith depends from beginning to end."

Eyes fixed on Jesus.

As we do so, a powerful behavioral law that Paul tells about in 2 Corinthians 3:18 goes to work: By beholding we are changed. As guidelines for lifestyle choices we then gladly accept Bible requirements such as the following:

- "Do you not know that your body is the temple of the Holy Spirit . . . ? For you were bought at a price; therefore glorify God in your body and in your spirit, which are God's" (1 Cor.6:19, 20).
- "Whether you eat or drink, or whatever you do, do all to the glory of God" (1 Cor. 10:31).

A degree in the science of prayer?

I read somewhere about a seminary at which students could get a degree in prayer. Should our colleges and universities offer enough courses on faith and prayer that students could get a degree in how to pray effectively? Should secondary and elementary schools also give instruction that would motivate children and youth to pray?

At the schools of the prophets prayer was a priority in the curriculum. "Not only were students taught the duty of prayer, but they were taught how to pray, how to approach their Creator, how to exercise faith in Him, and how to understand and obey the teachings of His Spirit" (*Patriarchs and Prophets*, 594).

You'll recall that chapters 10 and 11 of this book discussed finding something new in God's Word each day. The next sentence in the statement just quoted added, "Sanctified intellects brought forth from the treasure house of God things new and old."

The "sanctified intellects" must have included students as well as teachers. Can you imagine the excitement in a classroom as both teachers and students shared their "something new" discoveries?

As I was writing this chapter, I saw a new beauty in Paul's statement in 1 Corinthians 6, "Your body is the temple of the Holy Spirit who is in you, whom you have from God, and you are not your own" (19).

Here's the first thing God impressed upon me: Since a temple is a sacred place, we can and should think of our body as a place where worship ought to be the first priority. Having the Holy Spirit within gives a radiance and beauty nothing else can.

Second, the Holy Spirit within is *a gift* "whom you [we] have from God." As youth pray for each other and as the rest of us pray for Generation X, we can and should ask God to do whatever it takes to help them long for a sense of the Holy Spirit's presence.

As I mingle with youth, these two facts have led me to add this prayer to my petitions for youth: "Lord Jesus, thank You for sending the Holy Spirit to fill human temples. I claim this young person as a temple for the Holy Spirit."

For enrichment of this chapter's content, consider these options:

- *Review the reasons behind unanswered prayer; then ask yourself, "Are there any*

changes needed in order for me to expect more answers to prayer?"
- *Read the chapter in* Steps to Christ *titled "The Privilege of Prayer." Underline and meditate on what you see as the most helpful statements.*
- *Work on developing the habit of praying that God will work to make every child and young person in your local church a temple for an indwelling Holy Spirit. For encouragement as you do this, review Luke 11:1-13.*

16

Questions About Prayer

"Then He spoke a parable to them, that men always ought to pray and not lose heart" (Luke 18:1).

"If God is all good, then he is not all powerful. If God is all powerful, then he is not all good," said Norman Mailer, author of *The Gospel According to the Son*. "I am a disbeliever in the omnipotence of God because of the Holocaust," he added, "but for 35 years or so, I have been believing that he is doing the best he can" (cited in *Time*, 5 May 1997, 23).

What's behind this kind of doubt? Could it be a failure to understand what Revelation 12 and books such as *The Great Controversy* reveal about the battle between good and evil?

Picture yourself and Jesus as visiting together in your living room. He invites you to ask anything you want about prayer. What would you ask?

Space allows us to examine only a sample of questions. We'll start with one related to Mailer's concern:

1. **"Why does a God of love allow injustice and hate and war? How can He let little children starve to death? Where was God during the Holocaust?"**

Variations of these questions come up repeatedly. In his book *Disappointment With God* Philip Yancey quotes from a letter that was written by a mother who lost two children to cystic fibrosis. After a twenty-three-year-old daughter had died she said, "I was sitting by her bed a few days before her death when suddenly she began screaming. I will never forget those shrill, piercing, primal screams."

God could have helped, she added. But instead He "looked down upon a young woman devoted to Him, quite willing to die for Him to give Him glory, and decided to sit on His hands and let her death top the horror charts for cystic fibrosis deaths" (Philip Yancey, *Disappointment With God.* Grand Rapids, Mich.: Zondervan Publishing House, 1988, 158).

As we try to make sense out of tragedies, we need to remember that we live in what Jeremiah called "the land of the enemy" (Jer. 31:16). Jesus told a parable in which someone sowed weeds in a wheat field (Matt. 13:24-30). "An enemy has done this," the owner told his servants.

Many people are unaware of the fact that the battle between good and evil is much bigger than the conflict here on earth. They know nothing of Lucifer's rebellion against the authority of God and of His law or of his claim that if he were running things he would bring the inhabitants of the universe a greater happiness by abolishing what he called unneeded restraints. Because of his high position, and because he used flattery and deceit, Lucifer convinced one-third of the angels to join his rebellion (Rev. 12:4). For the future security of the universe, God has had to give Satan a chance to demonstrate whether or not doing away with God's law would bring greater happiness.

It has been necessary to allow sin to demonstrate what lawlessness is like. But this we know: Rebellion against God "will not come a second time" (Nahum 1:9, RSV). And even though we're still in the land of the enemy, Scripture assures us: "In all things God works for the good of those who love him" (Rom. 8:28, RSV). When an unexpected tragedy comes, we, too, can say, "An enemy did this." And in the resurrection the God of all comfort will make it right with us.

More questions

The following is another question often asked:

2. God already knows what I need. Why tell Him what He already knows?

God does know our every need. But it's also true that as human beings we tend to become self-sufficient and proud. One reason God wants us to ask is that asking helps us remember our dependence upon Him.

On the Thursday night before His crucifixion Jesus had the disciples gather around a grapevine. "Separate a branch from the vine," He said, "and it will dry up and be burned. If you become self-important and forget your dependence on Me, you, too, will become dry and fruitless" (paraphrased from John 15:1-60).

"The first lesson to be taught," Ellen White suggested, "is the lesson of dependence on God" (*Sons and Daughters of God,* 77). Prayer keeps us reminded of that dependence.

3. How can I know if what I am asking God for is His will?

The first thing to check is this: What does the Bible say that might apply to this request? What Bible principles apply?

At times God also guides by providences—shut doors, open doors. These, however, should always be compared with the teaching of Scripture.

Check, also, with godly friends. Get their thinking. If you are praying about a problem, try to find a solution-oriented friend to counsel with.

As you think and pray, be open to the leading of the Holy Spirit. Seek the Spirit's input by asking questions such as these: "Will what I'm asking bring honor to God? Might it come between me and God, or will it draw me closer to Him? Is it in the best interest of my spouse or of our children?"

4. If I'm pretty sure something is God's will, why keep on asking and asking? Shouldn't one request be sufficient?

When we ask for what we suppose is God's will, there may still be some of what Jeremiah calls a heart that "is deceitful above all things, and desperately wicked" (Jer. 17:9) that influences our desires.

One time a man complained to Martin Luther, "None of my wishes come true. My hopes go wrong. My plans never work out."

"My dear friend, that is your own fault," said Luther.

"My own fault?"

"Yes," said Luther. "When you pray 'Thy will be done,' in your heart you are praying, '*My* will be done.' "

Prayer does not change God—it changes us. We may need to search our hearts and repent of sin. As we keep bringing our requests, the Holy Spirit has opportunity to lead us to repentance and to truly seek His will rather than our own.

5. If I go without food, will God be more likely to answer my prayers?

No merit is earned by fasting. Yet in the Bible fasting and prayer are sometimes mentioned together (Dan. 9:3; Mark 9:29, KJV). As outward evidence of repentance, the people of Nineveh fasted in sackcloth and ashes (Jonah 3:5-10). David speaks of humbling himself by fasting (Ps. 35:13).

In His wilderness fast Christ totally abstained from food. Another type of fasting consists of eating less or omitting desserts. On one occasion Daniel simply abstained for three weeks from what he called "pleasant bread" (Dan. 10:3, KJV). Before God gave the Ten Commandments at Sinai, Moses asked husbands and wives to exercise self-denial by abstaining from sex during that time (Exod. 19:15). Paul suggested something similar when he wrote to the Corinthians: "Do not deprive one another except with consent for a time, so that you may give yourselves to fasting and prayer" (1 Cor. 7:5).

Here's a verse that implies another kind of fast: "So let us stop criticizing one another" (Rom. 14:13, Moffatt). Try going for a day—better still a week—without one word of criticism about anyone. Other possibilities include: a "worry fast" (no worry for a week); a "television fast" (a week with no TV).

During the "television fast," you might add that amount of time to your allotment for Bible study and prayer.

6. How can I keep my mind from wandering when I pray?

Try writing your prayer. One possibility: Write out a brief prayer using the acronym ACTS (adoration, confession, thanksgiving, supplication). Write a few sentences of adoration and of confession and of thanksgiving. Conclude with your requests. Then take that prayer and read it to God. Keep these prayers in some kind of notebook, and as God answers, record the date and how He answered.

This helps to develop what Ellen White calls "unlimited confidence in God" (*In Heavenly Places*, 71). A pastor of my acquaintance who does this says, "If my faith wavers, I just look at my record of prayers that God answered during the previous thirty or sixty days."

- *Do you ever wonder why tragedies happen, or why God allows things like the Holocaust? If so, you will find it helpful to read or review the chapter in* The Great Controversy *titled "Why Was Sin Permitted?"*
- *Which of the several kinds of fasting mentioned under question 5 would be the most beneficial to you? Select one and give it a try.*
- *Under question 2 we noted that "the first lesson to be taught is the lesson of dependence on God" (*Sons and Daughters of God, *77). If you were a pastor—or if you are—how might you teach this to your congregation?*

17

Praying for Adventist Leaders

"We . . . do not cease to pray for you" (Col. 1:9).

The 1997 *Yearbook* includes this information: Our denomination has nearly 41,000 congregations, led by some 12,000 pastors. The world field has 443 conferences and missions, grouped into ninety-two unions, arranged into twelve divisions. Several months ago, as a basis for a prayer to use collectively in behalf of Adventist leadership, I memorized the following:

> We . . . do not cease to pray for you, and to ask that you may be filled with the knowledge of His will in all wisdom and spiritual understanding; that you may have a walk worthy of the Lord, fully pleasing Him, being fruitful in every good work and increasing in the knowledge of God; strengthened with all might, according to His glorious power, for all patience and longsuffering with joy; giving thanks to the Father who has qualified us to be partakers of the inheritance of the saints in the light (Col. 1:9-12).

I wrote the above sentence on a 3 by 5 card that I kept with me until I had mastered it. Currently I use it collectively every day and often several times a day for Adventist leaders of the entire world field.

If hundreds of us would use prayers such as this one when praying for pastors and conference officials and for leaders in our schools, hospitals, publishing houses, and other ministries, the results would be immeasurable.

Leadership bashing

Just about every leader today, from the President of the United States to local officials, gets subjected to unfair and sometimes cruel criticism. In an article in the South Bend *Tribune*—"Degrading a President No Service to the Country"—Howard Klienberg, of the Cox News Service, cited examples of bashings that included every president from John Kennedy until now.

"Like a snowball rushing down a mountainside," Klienberg wrote, "the degrading of the presidency of the United States has gotten bigger than the mountain."

Far too often leaders within our own denomination are unfairly bashed. At times Ellen White herself was severely criticized. And leaders, whether political or denominational, have shortcomings. But, as Paul urged in 1 Timothy 2:1-4, above all else they need our "supplications, prayers, intercessions, and giving of thanks" (1).

It used to be that bashing of leaders came mostly from a few ultraconservative independent ministries. Now more of it seems to come from liberal elements in the church. And tragically, sometimes the liberals include a few pastors. As we pray for pastors and denominational leadership, we do well to plead with God for men and women who are a balance between the two extremes.

The basic request in Colossians 1:9-12 is this: that God grant the Colossians to "be filled with the knowledge of His will in all wisdom and understanding" (9). That's the place to begin as we pray for pastors and leaders, and for God to give them the balance all need. As God answers our prayers in their behalf the following will be the results:

1. **"A walk worthy of the Lord, fully pleasing Him."** I repeatedly ask God to give our leaders this kind of walk. I do the same for Adventist youth, and for their teachers.

2. **Fruitfulness in every good work.** Fruitfulness requires a total dependence on the One who said, "Without Me you can do nothing" (John 15:5). Fruitfulness comes *only* from abiding in Christ, and from His presence within. In prayers for leaders, youth, or whoever, one could linger on this point for some time.

3. **An increased knowledge of God.** I see this knowledge, first of all, as knowledge of the Scriptures *and* knowledge of the Spirit of Prophecy books. Every one of the nine volumes of *Testimonies for the Church*, for example, are commentaries that draw rich lessons from hundreds of Bible truths.

When teaching a class at the seminary about how to develop a rich prayer life, I give students a list of several dozen articles from which they can read samples. Volume 5, for example, includes these three messages: "Looking Unto Jesus," "Christian Growth," and "Praise Ye the Lord." Volume 7 includes "Family Worship," "Faith and Courage," and "Take Time to Talk With God."

In one chapter in my *Whatever It Takes Praying*, I included titles for twelve such messages. In 1996, John Kerbs, president of Union College, said he used some of his devotional time to read *Whatever It Takes Praying*. He wrote that when he got to the chapter with the list of these twelve messages from the *Testimonies*, he had read all of them.

In praying for our leaders and pastors, we would do well to pray that their love for the Bible and for the Spirit of Prophecy books will increase "still more and more." We can also pray, both for ourselves and them, for the discernment that Paul mentions in his Philippians 1:9-11 petition.

4. Strengthened with all might according to His glorious power for all patience and longsuffering with joy. The expression "glorious power" parallels a sentence from another of Paul's prayers. In Ephesians 3:16 Paul asked God to strengthen the Ephesians "with might through His Spirit in the inner man." He pleaded with God to do this "according to the riches of His glory" (Eph. 3:16).

What a treasure! Power and inner strength given "according to the riches of His glory"! As you pray for your pastor and for your conference president and other leaders, what richer gift could you ask?

5. Giving thanks to the Father who has qualified us to be partakers of the inheritance of the saints in the light. We do well to pray that God will help our leaders always to give thanks. We can ask God that as they seek to attract people to "the inheritance of the saints" their own appreciation of that inheritance will become more and more real.

More and still more!

After I had used the four verses of Colossians 1:9-12 for a time, I added the sentence that immediately follows:

> He has delivered us from the power of darkness and translated us into the kingdom of the Son of His love, in whom we have redemption through His blood, the forgiveness of sins (Col. 1:13, 14).

I love the way Paul brings the blood of Christ into focus! The closer one lives to Christ, the more one develops a keen awareness that, like Paul, we are the "chief" of sinners (1 Tim. 1:15). But Christ's blood, claimed by faith, brings "the forgiveness of sins."

In a leadership position one needs much "patience and longsuffering." If impatience trips us up—or self-confidence, pride, indiscretion, or whatever—we desperately need the blessings available through faith in Christ's blood; namely, (1) repentance and confession and (2) God's assurance of forgiveness.

In his book *Incredible Answers to Prayer*, Roger Morneau wrote that every day he turns to the crucifixion scenes of Matthew 27 for meditation.

Late in the summer of 1997 I went through that chapter looking for the word *blood*. Here's what I found:

Blood is mentioned three times in the opening verses. In his confession Judas said he had betrayed "innocent blood" (4), the chief priests called the coins returned by Judas "the price of blood" (6), and the burial plot they purchased became know as "the Field of Blood" (6, 8).

As he washed his hands Pilate said, "I am innocent of the blood of this just Person," to which the angry crowd screamed, "His blood be on us and on our children" (24, 25). I circled the word *blood* in each of these five verses.

The next verse, however, states: "When he had scourged Jesus, he delivered Him to be crucified" (26). That horrible scourging lacerated His back and even portions of His stomach, causing profuse bleeding. I wrote the word *blood* in the margin.

I did the same with verses 29 and 30, where soldiers "twisted a crown of thorns" on His head and then took a stick and slammed it down on the thorn crown. That produced intense pain and more blood.

The last mention is this statement, "Then they crucified Him" (35). Again, I wrote *blood* in the margin. I recalled this statement from *The Desire of Ages*:

> Heaven viewed with grief and amazement Christ hanging upon the cross, blood flowing from His wounded temple, and sweat tinged with blood standing upon His brow. From His hands and feet the blood fell, drop by drop, upon the rock drilled for the foot of the cross (760).

Almost every day I either open my Bible to Matthew 27 or recall the eight times the word *blood* is on that page and especially claim that blood in behalf of two groups: the children and youth of the church and our denomination's leaders.

Will you join me in praying for your local pastor, the leaders in your conference, and in a collective way for all leaders in all 12 of our world divisions, all 443 conferences, and all the 12,000 pastors caring for 41,000 local congregations? If so, you might also:

- *Write Colossians 1:9-12 on a 3 by 5 card and keep the card with you as you pray.*
- *Spend some time with Matthew 27 and circle the word* blood *in verses 4, 6, 8, 24, and 25. Then look for the statements that mention the scourging, the crown of thorns, and the crucifixion and write blood in the margin by each of these also.*
- *If you have access to volume 5 of the* Testimonies, *you'd enjoy reading one or more of these three chapters: "Looking to Jesus," "Christian Growth," "Praise Ye the Lord."*

18

Causing Satan to Tremble

**"Then the king said to me, 'What do you request?'
So I prayed to the God of heaven" (Neh. 2:4).**

Nehemiah didn't record what he said. It couldn't have been much. With King Artaxerxes intently staring at him, he probably didn't even close his eyes.

In the few seconds he had, Nehemiah may have simply breathed an "O God, help me" before he told the king, "If it please the king, and if your servant has found favor in your sight, I ask that you send me to Judah, to the city of my fathers' tombs, that I may rebuild it" (Neh. 2:4, 5).

As he prayed, Nehemiah had pressed into the presence of the King of kings, and won to his side the One who had said, "The king's heart is in the hand of the Lord" (Prov. 21:1). That five-second prayer changed the course of history in the Middle East.

There's something for NET '98 and our entry into a new millennium in Nehemiah's account of the rebuilding of the walls of Jerusalem, for he relied on prayer again and again. Almost all of chapter 1 is a prayer. Nehemiah's nighttime survey of the wall in chapter 2 must have included much prayer. Prayer gets mentioned twice in chapter 4 and again in chapter 6.

In chapter 8 Nehemiah's friend Ezra "blessed the Lord" and the people "bowed their heads and worshiped" (Neh. 8:6). Thirty-four of the thirty-eight verses in chapter 9 record a prayer. The dedication of the wall in chapter 12 included praise and prayer, and the last verse of the book is a prayer.

I found two Ellen White statements In the *SDA Bible Commentary* that sound like they were written for *right now!*

- "There is need of Nehemiahs in the church today—not men who can pray and preach only, but men whose prayers are braced with firm and eager purpose" (3:1137).

  Prayers braced with firm and eager purpose. Will you join me in asking God to raise up tens of thousands who will pray for NET '98 and beyond "with firmand eager purpose"?

- "His holy purpose, his high hope, his cheerful consecration to the work, were contagious. The people caught the enthusiasm of their leader, and in his sphere each man became a Nehemiah, and helped to make stronger the hand and heart of his neighbor" (ibid.).

His optimism and cheerful enthusiasm were contagious. The word *enthusiasm* comes from two Greek words, *en,* or in, and *theos,* God. May God give us thousands with that kind of contagious enthusiasm!

Causing Satan to tremble

Consider another example of the difference prayer can make: In 1863, as the Civil War (1861–1865) raged, Seventh-day Adventists organized into a 3,000, member denomination. Believers then, like now, often did very little praying, and Ellen White repeatedly emphasized that prayer can make a tremendous difference.

Some had circulated the theory that prayer does no good. In a chapter titled "Philosophy and Vain Deceit" Ellen White pointed out, "Satan leads many to believe that prayer to God is useless" (*Testimonies,* 1:295). In that 1862 message, as examples of "fervent, effectual prayer," she spoke of Elijah and Daniel and declared: "Satan is enraged at the sound of fervent prayer, for he knows that he will suffer loss" (ibid.*).* And again: "The name of Jesus, our Advocate, he detests; and when we earnestly come to Him for help, Satan's host is alarmed" (ibid., 296).

Later that year, in a message that focused on Christ as "the mighty Conqueror," the same author declared, "When they humbly entreat the mighty Conqueror for help, the weakest believer in the truth, relying firmly upon Christ, can successfully repulse Satan and all his host" (ibid., 341).

Near the end of that same message Ellen White put her encouragement to pray in startling words: "Satan cannot endure to have his powerful rival appealed to, for he fears and trembles before His strength and majesty. At the sound of fervent prayer Satan's whole host trembles" (ibid., 346).

When you ask Jesus for help, Satan doesn't just get nervous. He trembles. So do his angels. In the context of the above statement, Ellen White does not refer to a Daniel but to a new convert who has been a "captive" of Satan (ibid. 345). The context reveals something else we need to realize as we move into NET '98 and beyond: We are at war!

When Satan is about to lose one of his captives he "will call to his aid legions of his angels to oppose the advance of even one soul, and, if possible, wrest it from the hand of Christ" (ibid.). Yet, and this is incredibly wonderful, if the former captive of Satan goes to God in fervent prayer, *Satan's whole host trembles.*

The writer doesn't say whether Satan trembles because of rage or because he's actually terrified. Perhaps it's some of both. But ask yourself: "Do I really believe it? Am I taking time every day to pray so earnestly that Satan actually trembles?"

More terror for Satan

On this late September day my fall 1997 Workshop in Prayer class met for the second time. I had assigned students to read the first two chapters of Roger Morneau's *Incredible Answers to Prayer* and mark ideas they wanted to remember.

In chapter 1 Morneau had written, "I learned to fortify myself in the merits of the sacrificial blood of Christ. And in addition, I made it a part of my morning devotions to review the events of that sacrifice by reading Matthew 27:24-54. Such practices have removed all fear of the destroyer, and served to surround me with a spiritual atmosphere of light and peace" (17).

When I asked for examples, Rhonda, a young Lebanese woman, said she had been really touched by Mr. Morneau's reliance on the blood of Christ. Rhonda then read to the class this prayer from chapter 2:

> Our Father in heaven, I plead the merits of the precious blood of Christ shed on Calvary as the reason that I should receive help in the warfare against evil. By the mighty power of the Holy Spirit working in my behalf, please save me this day from self, from sin, from the world, and from the power of evil angels. Save me from self, by removing from my heart distrust and unbelief, and replace it by a living faith in Thee, so I can take Thee at Thy word. Thank You, Lord, for Your grace and Your love (27).

"I intend," Rhonda said, "to write this prayer on a 3 by 5 card and memorize it so I can use it too."

Mention of Christ's blood has a devastating effect on Satan. Volume 5 of the *Testimonies* contains a letter, "Praise Ye the Lord," written to a discouraged couple of the 1880s. In it Ellen White suggested, "When Satan would fill your mind with despondency, gloom, and doubt, resist his suggestions. Tell him of the blood of Jesus, that cleanses from all sin. You cannot save yourself from the tempter's power, but he trembles and flees when the merits of that precious blood are urged" (317).

The tempter trembles and flees when the merits of that precious blood are urged! As we try to take greater advantage of that almost stunning truth, consider these suggestions:

- *During your devotional time for the next week read at least a few verses from Matthew 27 and ask yourself three questions about what you have read: "What is there to see? What is there to hear? What is there to feel?"*
- *If you aren't already doing so, in your prayers for others mention the blood of Christ as your reason for seeking grace and mercy.*

19

Whatever It Takes

"Let this mind be in you which was also in Christ Jesus" (Phil. 2:5).

"I have to do this thing," the injured mountain climber said to himself. "Whatever it takes, I have to do it."

It was August 1, 1992. Climbing guides Scott Fischer and Ed Viesturs, from Seattle, Washington, had determined to reach the top of Himalayan K2—the second highest mountain in the world and the hardest to climb. Previous attempts to reach the top of its 28,250-foot summit had already cost thirty-three lives.

Fischer and Viesturs climbed as tied-together partners. Shortly after they left base camp at 20,000 feet, an ice chunk shifted and threw Fischer off balance. "Falling!" he screamed. As he landed in a narrow chasm, a sharp pain stabbed his right shoulder. His arm had been pulled out of its socket. After a physician in the group had jerked Fischer's arm back into the socket he told him, "For you the trip is over."

Fischer stayed in camp for two weeks, but when two Russians reached the top on August 1, Fischer made a decision. Even with a bad arm he would resume the climb. "Whatever it takes," he told Viesturs as they left base camp.

They had to struggle with an avalanche that wrenched Fischer's bad arm, but they finally got 2,000 feet from the summit. The pain in his arm became still worse, but again he said, "I've got to go for it, whatever it takes." They started at 1:30 a.m. and reached the summit at noon. After taking fifty-three days to get there, they stayed only thirty-five minutes.

There's a tragic footnote. The cover story in the May 27, 1996 *Newsweek* magazine, titled "Trapped on Everest," told of the deaths of eight of the thirty-one climbers who had made it to the summit of Everest on Friday, May 10. Fischer had led one of the five expeditions that reached the summit, and was among the eight who perished in a storm that sent temperatures forty degrees below zero.

Out in eternity

Whatever it takes! At a "counsel of peace" (Zech. 6:13, KJV) the three intergalactic executives who run the universe made history's first "whatever it takes" decision. When Lucifer rebelled, God made many attempts at reconciliation but finally had to expel him from heaven. Satan had access to the newly created Adam and Eve and persuaded them to also disobey God. For a moment, imagine that you are God. What would you have done with Adam and Eve?

You could slap their wrists and tell them, "Just don't do it again." But that would have undermined your administration; laws that are circumvented become worthless. And if you did destroy Adam and Eve, along with Lucifer with his followers, seeds of fear would have been planted in hearts of your subjects.

Satan figured that he had the government of heaven stymied. "Eventually," he told himself, "I will get other worlds to join my rebellion."

With a single breath you could wipe out all opposition and keep on doing so. But would you want to operate a universe like that? God didn't.

A "whatever it takes" plan

What God did do was call the above-mentioned "counsel of peace." At that meeting love took over—love for Adam and Eve, love for their descendants, and love for the unfallen worlds. Nothing more could be done for Lucifer and his fallen angels; they had gone too far. But there was hope for Adam and Eve, and Christ suggested a plan.

"The violation of law cannot be ignored," He said. "The wages of sin is death and that penalty must be paid. But I will pay it. I will become a man, live among human beings, and seek to win back their allegiance. Then I will pay the penalty by dying on a cross. All who accept that sacrifice can be forgiven and through study of the Word will be transformed."

The Father and the Holy Spirit would also do *whatever it takes* to save a fallen planet. And they would do it even though this planet is only a tiny speck in a universe of hundreds of billions of galaxies!

Satan had claimed that the Trinity were self-serving. But as he watched the sacrificial system and figured out what Heaven had in mind, it flabbergasted him. He couldn't understand that kind of sacrifice. He determined to fight against it, but in his heart he must have realized he would fail.

Why did the Trinity do it?

Love. Every human being matters! Each is loved! Each has infinite value! "You were not redeemed with corruptible things, like silver or gold," Peter writes, "but with the precious blood of Christ" (1 Peter 1:18, 19). Your value and that of each of your friends and neighbors equals the worth of the blood of Christ! That surpasses the real estate value of ten thousand worlds!

Do we even begin to realize how valuable our children and friends and neighbors are to Christ? Are we willing to do *whatever it takes* to win them?

"Whatever it takes," of course, must always be within the constraints of God's Word. That precludes any violation of integrity. It bars excessive labor and neglect of home and family. At the same time, it motivates intense prayer and fervent faith.

"Whatever it takes" praying

The first place for *whatever it takes* is in our prayer life. Paul's prayers for the youthful Timothy illustrate the sense of urgency we do well to develop in praying for our children, our friends, and for Adventist youth everywhere.

As he sat in a Roman prison, Paul penned the last letter he would ever write. In it he told the young Timothy that "without ceasing I remember you in my prayers night and day" (2 Tim. 1:3).

The Message paraphrase reads: "Every time I say your name in prayer—which is practically all the time—I thank God for you. . . . I miss you a lot, especially when I remember that last tearful goodbye, and I look forward to a joy-packed reunion" (2 Tim. 1:3, 4).

That "joy-packed reunion" is still future. Shortly after Paul wrote 2 Timothy, Nero ordered his death. But Paul's prayers for Timothy and for all of his converts are still bearing fruit as others continue to imitate his example.

Another awesome prayer to use

Would you consider writing another Bible prayer on a 3 by 5 card to use as you pray? Here's a short but really powerful one: "Blessed be the Lord God, the God of Israel, who only does wondrous things! And blessed be His glorious name forever! And let the whole earth be filled with His glory. Amen and Amen" (Ps. 72:18, 19).

What are you asking when you pray, "Let the whole earth be filled with His glory"? In John 1:14 the author of that gospel said, "The Word became flesh, and dwelt among us, and we beheld His glory . . . full of grace and truth." Doesn't this show that Christ's glory is His character? And doesn't God want each of His children to reflect that glory? In Psalm 112:4 David wrote this about the person who loves and fears God: "He is gracious, and full of compassion, and righteous."

I have taken the petition "Let the whole earth be filled with His glory" and rephrased it: *Let the whole earth—every nation, tribe, tongue, and people— be filled with believers and with new converts who reflect the glory of Your character.*

Isn't that what we want for NET '98 and for every effort, to let people know about the One who is "full of grace and truth"? David's petition is so simple that I can pray it many times a day just in my coming and going.

Both for personal security in Christ and for use in praying for others, never forget this promise: "If we walk in the light as He is the light . . . The blood of Jesus Christ His Son cleanses us from all sin" (1 John 1:7). In the context of that assurance, let praise to God fill our hearts for this previously mentioned assurance that has been printed in sixteen different places in the writings of Ellen White:

> "Nothing is apparently more helpless, yet really more invincible, than the soul that feels its nothingness and relies wholly on the merits of the Saviour. God would send every angel in heaven to the aid of such a one, rather than allow him to be overcome" (*Sons and Daughters of God*, 35).

Will you join me in relying totally upon the merits of Christ as you intercede for others?

- *Ask God to give you, and all His people, a heart that feels compassion for the lost. In that compassion let's memorize, "Let the whole earth be filled with Your glory." Then try this experiment: During the next twenty-four hours, with yearning compassion, send that brief petition heavenward as many times as you can.*
- *As often as you think of it, blend into your prayers a total reliance upon the fact that the blood of Christ brings both forgiveness and transformation.*

20

Seeking the Lost

**" 'Rejoice with me, for I have found
my sheep which was lost' " (Luke 15:6).**

A few yards offshore a woman floundered among the chunks of ice in the river. A helicopter had let down a life preserver, but it had slipped from her hands. The pilot made a second attempt, but she did not have the strength to grasp it.

Millions watched as TV cameras picked up the rescue attempts after Air Florida Flight 90 had plunged into the Potomac River at Washington's Fourteenth Street bridge. Viewers saw the look of helpless terror in the woman's eyes.

A group of rescue workers and onlookers stood along the riverbank. Suddenly a young man broke away from them and plunged into the river. With strong strokes he swam toward the woman. He got to where she was, seized her, and turned toward the shore. A man with a rope rushed forward to meet them, and soon the woman was on the snowy riverbank.

Lenny Skutrik had saved the life of Priscilla Tirado.

Lenny, a twenty-eight-year-old messenger at the Congressional Budget Office, had been let off work early that snowy afternoon of January 13, 1982. As he made his way home he came to the terror just off Washington's Fourteenth Street bridge. Along with ambulances and helicopters he saw passengers bobbing in the icy water. He stopped his car and joined the crowd on the riverbank. But unlike the others, he slipped off his coat and boots and dived in.

He became an instant hero. Asked why he plunged into a freezing river, at dusk, in a snowstorm, he replied, "If I hadn't done it, she would have died."

It's hard to imagine any delight greater than the joy of saving an individual from physical death. But what about the thrill of being the instrument God uses to save someone from eternal death?

Laborers together with God

As you pray for and minister to others, you become what Paul called "laborers together with God" (1 Cor. 3:9, KJV). And as your prayers and witness help another person find Christ, God rejoices with you.

In Ephesians, Paul's "prayer epistle," he wrote this:

> Therefore I also, after I heard of your faith in the Lord Jesus and your love for all the saints, do not cease to give thanks for you, making mention of you in my prayers, that the God of our Lord Jesus Christ, the Father of glory, may give to you the spirit of wisdom and revelation in the knowledge of Him (Eph. 1:15-17).

Note what Paul requested for the Ephesians: *the spirit of wisdom and revelation in the knowledge of Him.* He goes on to tell what the results will be: "the eyes of your understanding being enlightened, that you may know what is the hope of His calling, what are the riches of the glory of His inheritance in the saints, and what is the exceeding greatness of His power toward us who believe" (Eph. 1:18, 19).

I am intrigued by the expression "the riches of the glory of His inheritance in the saints." Christ's inheritance is people redeemed by His blood. When we join Him in seeking the lost, and claim the blood of Christ in their behalf, we share that inheritance and even now begin to enter into His joy.

Near the close of chapter 17 we went to Matthew 27 and noted five mentions of the word *blood* in that chapter. Did you go to there and circle the five mentions of Christ's *blood*? And in the statements where Christ was scourged, then had a crown of thorns slammed down on His head, and then was crucified, did you write *blood* in the margin of your Bible next to the description of those three scenes?

At the time of this writing I have been claiming Christ's blood in behalf of the lost for several weeks. It has become such a habit that even in my coming and going I am learning to go to Matthew 27 as a "mighty argument" in behalf of those for whom I am praying. And it's really making a difference. More than ever before I have seen numerous providences, leadings, and opportunities to minister.

For example, I'm the community services director at the Coloma church, one of the two I pastored before retiring. Two days ago a single parent who had lost her job when her car failed called to ask for some food. When I delivered it yesterday, her nine-year-old son Michael needed air in one of his bicycle tires. I took him and his bicycle to a station to get air, and as we talked, I found out that he has thought of becoming a pastor.

I left him and his sister two "Your Story Hour" tapes, and since they are nonchurch people, my wife and I are going to try to reach the mother through tapes and Bible stories for the children. And without fail, from now on I will be going to Matthew 27 as I pray for Michael and his eleven-year-old sister Megan.

Last winter Pastor Dwight Nelson gave a talk in which he called attention to this cry of the people in Matthew 27: "His blood be on us and on our children" (25). It was screamed out as a curse, he said, but we can take that same statement and turn it into a prayer. As we pray for ourselves, for our children, for the youth of the church, and for lost people, we can pray, "Your blood, Lord Jesus, be on us and on our children."

Satan recalls with terror his failure at Calvary, and he flees when we mention Christ's blood as our right to make bold requests. Let's keep him fleeing as we claim the merits of Christ for ourselves and for lost people.

Eternity's embraces

When the wonder-filled future described in Revelation 21 and 22 becomes reality, God wants each of us to be within the group described here:

> O what a scene of rejoicing it will be when the Lamb of God shall place upon the heads of the redeemed the victor's crown! Never, never more will you be led into temptation and sin. You will see the King in His beauty. And those you have helped heavenward will meet you there. They will throw their arms about you and acknowledge what you have done for them. "You watched over me," they will say; "you prayed for me; you helped me to gain heaven" (*In Heavenly Places*, 280).

The final two chapters of the Bible tell of Eden restored and of ever-increasing joy in what Micah called "the first dominion" (Micah 4:8, KJV). Some years ago, in *Counsels to Parents, Teachers, and Students*, I came to the chapter entitled "The Primal Object of Education." The message ends with this description of heaven:

> Through ceaseless ages to advance in wisdom, in knowledge, and in holiness, ever exploring new fields of thought, ever finding new wonders and new glories, ever increasing in capacity to know and to enjoy and to love, and knowing that still beyond us joy and love and wisdom infinite—such is the object to which the Christian hope is

pointing, for which Christian education is preparing (55).

What will it mean to keep discovering "new wonders and new glories" for all ages to come? What will it be like to keep growing *"in capacity to know and to enjoy and to love"*? How could heaven ever get dull when the future will include "joy and love and wisdom infinite"?

Pray, pray, pray, pray

I've mentioned *My Life Today* and *In Heavenly Places*. Similar books compiled from the writings of Ellen White have been published every third year since 1950. Yesterday I reviewed statements marked in *Reflecting Christ*. This sentence intrigued me: "The influence of the prayer of faith is as far-reaching as eternity" (102).

You may recall that in chapter 6 we summarized the evidence that every prayer backed by the merits of Christ is "placed upon heaven's imperishable record" to remain there for all eternity.

What an awesome thought! Every prayer you prayed last week has been put on heaven's "imperishable record" and will be there for all eternity! And the influence of every prayer will be just as lasting!

As I think of the future, I want to do as this suggests: "Make God your entire trust. Pray, pray, pray, pray in faith. Trust then the keeping of your soul to God. . . . Trust fully, unwaveringly in God" (*Reflecting Christ*, 119).

Consider two suggestions:

- *Spend some time with Ephesians 1:15-23. You might want to mark the request Paul made for the Ephesians in verse 17 and what he expected God to do for them as given in verses 18 and 19. Consider asking God to do something similar for the people on your prayer list.*
- *Have you started writing a short passage of Scripture on a 3 by 5 card each day to carry with you and use with your prayers? If not, why not give it a try?*

21

Praying With Great Boldness

"God be merciful to us, and bless us, and cause His face to shine upon us, that Your way may be known on earth, Your salvation among all nations" (Ps. 67:1-3).

The stamps on Pauline's passport include places like Iraq, China, Egypt, Russia, Kenya, Cyprus, Honduras, Hong Kong, Belise, and Turkey. Her ministry, which focuses especially on children and youth, has taken her to forty-one countries. "I claim the children of the world as my children," she says.

Pauline Yoder, who was born into an Amish family, lives in Goshen, Indiana. When she was still a child, her parents left the Amish faith and joined a conservative Mennonite congregation. She made her first trip in 1974, when a student group from a Bible college in Ohio went to France to build a youth center and then to deliver Bibles and relief supplies to a Communist-bloc country.

Her love for children and youth illustrates our need as Seventh-day Adventists to develop a similar interest in and love for the children and youth of the entire world.

The wonder in Psalm 67

As I looked for a Scripture passage to memorize that parallels the mandate of Revelation 14:6 about getting salvation's message to all nations and peoples, I selected Psalm 67. It begins with a plea for mercy. The Israel of the Old Testament had failed God again and again and needed His mercy and forgiveness.

Immediately after asking for mercy and blessing, David tells why: "That

Your way may be known on the earth, Your salvation among all nations" (2).

Verse 3 suggests, "Let the peoples praise You, O God, let all the peoples praise you." Verse 4 urges "the nations" to be glad and sing for joy because God will judge righteously. Verse 5 again urges praise, after which Psalm 67 ends, "Then the earth shall yield her increase; God, our own God, shall bless us, and all the ends of the earth shall fear Him" (Ps. 67:6, 7).

Five things stand out that make Psalm 67 an especially powerful prayer to use in behalf of our world work:

- It begins with a plea for mercy (1).
- It twice speaks of getting the message of salvation to *all* peoples (2, 7).
- It mentions the judgment—an event in which God judges righteously. Psalm67 presents it as a reason for joy (4).
- It twice urges praise (3, 5).
- As His people praise Him, God causes the earth to yield its increase (5, 6).

Praying in groups

I found Psalm 67 easy to memorize, first writing it (as usual) on as 3 by 5 card that I carried in a shirt pocket until I had mastered it. In my private prayers I try to use it every day, and many times a day. I do so in the assurance, as we explored in chapter 6, that every sincere prayer has an eternal influence for good.

I also see it as a valuable addition to group prayers. Jesus directed attention to the power available through group prayer when He said: "Again I say to you that if two of you agree on earth concerning anything that they ask, it will be done for them by My Father in heaven. For where two or three are gathered together in My name, I am there in the midst of them" (Matt. 18:19, 20).

"When two of you get together on anything at all on earth and make a prayer of it," Eugene Peterson's The Message paraphrases verse 19 "my Father in heaven goes into action."

God has long wanted to "go into action" to fulfill the mandate of Revelation 14:6 and the promise of Revelation 18:1. To help bring that about He invites, "Ask the Lord for rain in the time of the latter rain. The Lord will make flashing clouds; He will give them showers of rain, grass in the field for everyone" (Zech. 10:1).

Consider a suggestion penned in 1895:

> The descent of the Holy Spirit upon the church is looked forward to as in the future, but it is the privilege of the church to have it now. Seek for it, pray for it, believe for it. We must have it, and Heaven is waiting to bestow it (*Evangelism*, 701).

"Seek for it, pray for it, believe for it." Isn't that what the Holy Spirit wants in preparation for NET '98 and beyond?

Seeking is defined by these words: "If My people, who are called by My name, will humble themselves, and pray, and seek My face, and turn from their wicked ways, then I will hear from heaven, and heal their land" (2 Chron. 7:14). Chapters 22–28 will explore how to meet the conditions mentioned here.

Praying must get top priority for us to experience latter-rain power. But seeking and praying require one more thing—*believing for it*. That's why we keep coming back to God's Word and His promises as a basis for a growing faith. As *My Life Today* puts it, "His promises . . . have no limit but our faith" (14).

Large, bold requests

As I memorized Paul's prayers, I began to realize that he loved to make bold, large requests. God invites us to do the same. In Hebrews 4, after a focus on the power of God's Word in verse 12 and upon Christ as our High Priest in verses 14 and 15, Paul urges, "Let us therefore come boldly to the throne of grace, that we may obtain mercy, and find grace to help in time of need" (Heb. 4:16).

I see this invitation as good for personal needs but equally important as we pray for denominational needs. We can come boldly and with worldwide requests.

At one time I didn't see much value in praying collectively for large groups or for an entire denomination. Then I came across the following about God knowing the name of each star: "He counts the number of the stars; He calls them all by name. Great is our Lord, and mighty in power; His understanding is infinite" (Ps. 147:4, 5).

God calls each star by name! That's at least one hundred billion stars just in our home-town Milky Way! These statements gave me new glimpses of God's awesome mental capability. I won't frustrate Him if I pray collectively for every believer in an entire division. Nor is He overwhelmed if I collectively pray for our 81 colleges, 930 academies, and 4,522 elementary schools in a single request.

Let me encourage you, also, to keep mentioning the blood of Christ as the basis for bold requests. Just through the process of writing this book, I have developed the habit of including mention of that blood with almost every request that relates to young people. I mention it when praying for a single individual and when using Philippians 1:9-11 or Psalm 67 and even with the Lord's Prayer. For example, "Because of the blood shed on Calvary, I pray that Your name will be hallowed *this very day* in the lives of every young Seventh-day Adventist."

Here are two suggestions that could help as you "ask" and "seek" and "knock":

• *What significance do you see in the prominence of praise in Psalm 67? You might* want to write Psalm 67 on a 3 by 5 card and begin to use it in your prayers for the global work of the church. You could thank God for what He has done, what He is doing, and what He is going to do in getting a knowledge of salvation to "all nations."

- For encouragement when you bring bold requests, it might be good to recall this assurance: "Every act of love, every word of kindness, every prayer in behalf of the suffering and oppressed, is reported before the eternal throne and placed on heaven's impereishable record" (My Life Today, 237).

22

An Amazing Answer to Prayer

"If My people, who are called by My name, will humble themselves, and pray, and seek My face, and turn from their wicked ways, then I will hear from heaven, and forgive their sin and heal their land" (2 Chron. 7:14).

Amaze means "to fill with great surprise or sudden wonder, to astonish." In this chapter our purpose is to increase faith through a story of an incredible deliverance. It illustrates two things: God's amazing grace toward His erring children and His ability to deliver when we humbly call upon Him.

At the start of his reign, Solomon had talked to God about problems that the nation might face—defeat before enemies, pestilence, famine, etc. In His answer, given above, God plainly tells His people what they would need to do to get His help. King Jehoshaphat of Judah cited parts from the preceding promise as he pleaded for deliverance at the time three powerful enemies had united for an attempt to destroy Judah.

Jehoshaphat reigned over Judah for twenty-five years and had done much that was right. "His heart took delight in the ways of the Lord" (2 Chron. 17:6). He removed images and sent teachers all through Judah to instruct the people in the law of God (2 Chron. 17:7-10).

Like us, he also made some bad decisions. He almost lost his life when he agreed to help Ahab in a battle against the Syrians—a story recorded in 2 Chronicles 18. The first verses of chapter 19 tell of Jehoshaphat's return to Jerusalem. A prophet named Jehu confronted the king to ask: "Should you help the wicked and love those who hate the Lord?" (2 Chron. 19:2).

The king did not become angry at this public reproof, and Jehu commended him for removing images from the land and for seeking God (3). The repentant Jehoshaphat "went out again among the people from Beersheba to the mountains of Ephraim, and brought them back to the Lord God of their fathers" (2 Chron. 19:4).

Seeking the Lord in prayer

Not long after the preceding reforms, King Jehoshaphat got this message: "A great multitude is coming against you from beyond the sea" (2 Chron. 20:2). Two powerful nations east of the Jordan, Moab and Ammon, had conspired with Edom to attack Judah.

Jehoshaphat "set himself to seek the Lord, and proclaimed a fast throughout all Judah. So Judah gathered together to ask help from the Lord, and from all the cities of Judah they came to seek the Lord" (2 Chron. 20:3, 4).

The king met with his people in the court of Solomon's temple. All Judah had come—the men, "their little ones, their wives, and their children" (13). Jehoshaphat offered a prayer that brought tears to many eyes. He ended with this appeal: "We have no power against this great multitude that is coming against us; nor do we know what to do, but our eyes are upon you" (12).

Imagine yourself as one of Jehoshaphat's troops, and among the crowd. As your king made this plea, what emotions would have surged through your heart?

After Jehoshaphat said "Amen!" the Spirit of the Lord came upon Jahaziel, a Levite. He encouraged them not to be afraid. "The battle is not yours, but God's," he said. "Tomorrow go down against them. . . . You will not need to fight in this battle. Position yourselves, stand still and see the salvation of the Lord, who is with you, O Judah and Jerusalem!" (15-17).

Victory!

As you and the thousands of other troops prepare to leave the next morning, the entire city is astir. You will head south out of Jerusalem toward the Dead Sea. But as you wait for the order to march, Jehoshaphat strides to the front of the troops and says, "Hear me, O Judah and you inhabitants of Jerusalem. Believe in the Lord your God, and you shall be established; believe His prophets, and you shall prosper" (2 Chron. 20:20).

You and your fellow soldiers fervently exclaim, "Amen! Amen!"

After consulting with advisors, Jehoshaphat "appointed those who should sing to the Lord, and who should praise the beauty of holiness, as they went out before the army and were saying: 'Praise the Lord, for His mercy endures forever' " (2 Chron. 20:21).

You find yourself among the leading members of the choir. With exultation you sing as you head toward the battlefield!

You get your first view of the enemy just as you reach "a place overlooking the wilderness" (2 Chron. 20:24), several miles north of Engedi. But an amazing thing has happened! Apparently the generals in each of the three nations have become confused. The troops of Ammon and Moab mistook the Edomites for Hebrews and attacked and slaughtered them.

Then, still confused, they have turned on each other. By the time you get close enough for a good view, you see only "dead bodies fallen on the earth. No one had escaped" (2 Chron. 20:24).

"When Jehoshaphat and his people came to take away their spoil, they found among them an abundance of valuables on the dead bodies" (25). It takes you and the other troops three days to gather up all the treasures (2 Chron. 20:25).

On the fourth day your commander-in-chief assembles his troops in a valley known ever after as "The Valley of Blessing." The entire army forms into a gigantic choir and sings praises to God. You try to forget the battlefield with its dead bodies. You praise God that you and your fellow troops didn't have to lift a sword.

"Then they returned, every man of Judah and Jerusalem, with Jehoshaphat in front of them, to go back to Jerusalem with joy, for the Lord had made them rejoice over their enemies. So they came to Jerusalem, with stringed instruments and harps and trumpets, to the house of the Lord" (2 Chron. 20:27-30).

Seeking the Lord today

What can we learn from this experience? I find that what this story reveals about God's mercy is reason for both courage and thanksgiving. If we are willing to be corrected, He will work with us in marvelous ways in spite of our mistakes.

Second, Judah's experience in seeking God encourages us to fervently seek the Lord. The promise at the start of this lesson shows what seeking God must include: humbling ourselves, praying, seeking God's face, and turning from all wicked ways.

We will devote the next several chapters to these four conditions. At this point I want to mention Randy Maxwell's book *If My People Pray.* It has been widely read and has blessed thousands. If you don't have it, you would do well to get it.

My next six chapters are written with the hope many youth and others will catch a vision of helping bring about a fulfillment of the Joel 2 prophecies. In Joel 2 the deep repentance of Joel 2:12-17 *precedes* the numerous latter rain prophecies in Joel 2:18-32.

Before reading further, you might want to compare the story of this chapter to your own needs. Consider these ideas:

- *Jehoshaphat made several bad mistakes. God, however, did not forsake him, and 2 Chronicles 20 records how wonderfully our forgiving God is able to help His repentant people. As this church nears a new millennium, what encouragement do you find in this record of God's mercy?*
- *Do you praise God when troubles arise? Read 2 Chronicles 20 and ask yourself, What does this story reveal about the power of praise?*

23

Revival and Reform: What and How?

"Will you not revive us again, that Your people may rejoice in You? Show us Your mercy, O Lord, and grant us Your salvation" (Ps. 85:6, 7).

What should revival and reform include? What kinds of changes do we need in our personal lives and in our church to bring our lifestyle into total harmony with God's will? What will it take to bring about the lifestyle changes—the reforms—that are always the result of true revival?

In 1887 Ellen White wrote, "A revival of true godliness among us is the greatest and most urgent of all our needs. To seek this should be our first work. There must be earnest effort to obtain the blessing of the Lord, not because God is not willing to bestow His blessing upon us, but because we are so unprepared to receive it" (*Selected Messages*, 1:121).

After a few words about God's willingness to give His Spirit, Ellen White adds, "But it is our work, by confession, humiliation, repentance, and earnest prayer, to fulfill the conditions upon which God has promised to grant us His blessing. A revival need be expected only in answer to prayer" (ibid.).

The preceding appeal, made in 1887, has been repeatedly cited in the *Review*, in sermons, and in books. Key ideas in its context include:

- Seeking God for revival and reform is an *individual* work—a work in which each searches his heart and puts away sin (ibid. 122).
- We have far more to fear from within than from without. Because of unbelief and sin, the professed advocates of truth are often the greatest obstacle to its advancement (ibid.).

- Every church member should live such a godly life that others will ask, "What makes these people so different?" (124).
- There is nothing Satan fears so much as that the people of God will remove every barrier so that God can give His Spirit in full measure (ibid.).
- When the way is prepared for the Spirit of God, the blessing will come. Satan can no more stop the latter rain that he can hold back literal rain showers (ibid.).

Living radiantly!

Isaiah, Joel, Hosea, and other Bible prophets make many appeals in which the application includes a focus on the last days. Here's one:

> Arise, shine; for your light has come! And the glory of the Lord has arisen upon you. For behold, the darkness shall cover the earth, and deep darkness the people; but the Lord will arise over you, and His glory will be seen upon you. The Gentiles shall come to your light, and kings to the brightness of your rising (Isa. 60:1-3).

The next seven verses tell of an ingathering of converts—sons and daughters brought "from afar" (4, 9). Isaiah declares to those sharing the gospel: "Then you shall see and become radiant, and your heart shall swell with joy" (5).

"When God's people so fully separate themselves from evil that He can let the light of heaven rest upon them in rich measure," Ellen White wrote, "and shine forth from them to the world, then there will be fulfilled more fully than it has ever been fulfilled in the past, the prophecy of Isaiah, in which the servant of God declared of the remnant church in the last days: 'The Gentiles shall come to thy light, and kings to the brightness of thy rising' " (*Review and Herald*, 31 March 1910, 3).

What prepares the way? God's people making a *total separation from evil.* Leaders and laymen take seriously the appeal to humble themselves and pray and seek God's face and turn from their wicked ways (2 Chron. 7:14). For doing this consider a few "whats" and "hows":

Health and revival

The Lord through His servant gave a 1900 message, in volume 6 of the *Testimonies,* entitled "A Revival in Health Reform." It's built from five Bible passages: the fact that our body is to be a temple for God's Spirit (1 Cor. 6:19, 20), the experience of Daniel and his friends (Daniel 1), the withholding of a flesh diet in the wilderness (Numbers 11), Paul's appeal to bring body desires "into subjection" and live temperately (1 Cor. 9:24-27), and a warning against "harmful lusts" (1 Tim. 6:9).

The mention of "harmful lusts" is in the context of the indulgence of appetite—a fault through which "the power to discern sacred things is to a great extent destroyed" (*Testimonies for the Church*, 6:374).

It's in the context of "selfish, health-destroying indulgences of men and women" that this strong declaration is made:

> The Lord does not now work to bring many souls into the truth, because of the church members who have never been converted, and those who were once converted but who have now backslidden. What influence would these unconsecrated members have on new converts? Would they not make of no effect the God-given message which His people are to bear? (ibid., 371).

Two pages later she added, "I know that many of our brethren are in heart and practice opposed to health reform." The word *brethren* would take in some of the leaders of that time.

More needed changes

What? An eagerness for God's Word similar to what Jeremiah experienced when he declared, "Your words were found, and I ate them, and Your word was to me the joy and rejoicing of my heart" (Jer. 15:16). "A revival of Bible study is needed throughout the world" (*Evangelism*, 456).

How? Life-changing Bible study takes two things. The first is a hunger and thirst for God: "I will pour water upon him who is thirsty," God promises, adding: "I will pour My Spirit on your descendants, and My blessing on your offspring" (Isa. 44:3).

The second necessity is to put Bible study into our daily schedules, and keep at it there, making it a habit. Private study is important, but small group study like that described in chapter 13 can bring an ever-increasing spirit of revival.

What? Exchange the dullness of a mundane Christian experience for a vibrant, joyous fellowship with Jesus.

How? One time as two Christians were admiring flowers in a well-kept garden, one asked the other, "What does Christ mean to you?" Pointing to some flowers, the other replied: "What the sun is to those flowers, Jesus Christ is to me."

For my life to be lighted with an indwelling Christ, I've got to regularly spend time reading and thinking about Him. A good way to do that is to read from the Gospels and *The Desire of Ages*. As you read a narrative, put yourself into the picture by asking "What is there to see? To hear? To feel?"

What? The need for all of us, as we start the day, is to make a full surrender to Jesus Christ.

How? In your mind go frequently to the foot of the Cross, and kneeling there give yourself totally and completely to Jesus. When assailed by temptation, try to reaffirm that surrender.

Here's a prayer, adapted from page 70 of *Steps to Christ,* that I pray almost every morning: "Take me, O Lord, as wholly Thine. I lay all my plans at Your feet. Use me today in Your service. Please abide with me, bless me, and make me a blessing this very day."

More assurances

Through Paul God assured His people that at the very end He would move swiftly. "For He will finish the work and cut it short in righteousness, because the Lord will make a short work upon the earth" (Rom. 9:28). Our part is to seek the divine power that will enable God to do so:

"When divine power is combined with human effort, the work will spread like fire in the stubble. God will employ agencies whose origin man will be unable to discern; angels will do a work which men might have had the blessing of accomplishing, had they not neglected to answer the claims of God" (*Selected Messages,* 1:118).

• *Would you be willing to join me in asking God to give Christian youth the kind of hunger and thirst for God's Word that will bring a revival of Bible study in their lives?*

• *How about selecting a specific country for which you try to pray every day? As you pray, be aware that every prayer you send up becomes a part of "heaven's imperishable record" and will be there for all eternity.*

24

If My People Humble Themselves

**"If My people, who are called by My name,
will humble themselves . . ." (2 Chron. 7:14).**

One time a college teacher scolded a student who had addressed her as Professor, and warned, "Don't ever again call me 'Professor.' I'm *Doctor* So and So."

People afflicted with Laodicea's pride seldom are that bold about their importance. Pride finds more subtle methods—name-dropping, driving status cars, buying expensive furnishings, adopting trendy styles, justification of a little jewelry, etc.

Have you ever wondered why humbling ourselves *precedes* the other requirements in God's message about how to have revival? Why does it come before prayer, before seeking God's face, and before turning from our wicked ways. Here are some things that I discovered:

- In Scripture the word *humble* does not imply self-depreciating; its primary meaning is "not proud, not self-assertive."
- God has a special regard for a person who has "a contrite and humble spirit" (Isa. 57:15).
- Two of history's greatest leaders, Moses and Paul, were both humble men, but they were also men who firmly confronted evil.
- Our precious Saviour rules billions of galaxies yet said of Himself, "I am gentle and lowly in heart" (Matt. 11:29). When placed in contrast to Him, our human pride of position, wealth, accomplishment, or whatever, stands out in stark contrast.

- It is only through beholding Christ and kneeling at the foot of the Cross that we can become truly humble (2 Cor. 3:18).

Humility generally is accompanied by a quiet dignity and tends to be kind, thoughtful, and caring. That gentle, self-forgetful spirit adds much charm to one's personality.

Laodicea's self-importance

Note this statement in Revelation 3 about the offensiveness of the pride and self-importance found in the Laodicean remnant:

> I know your works, that you are neither cold nor hot. I could wish you were cold or hot. So then, because you are lukewarm, and neither cold nor hot, I will spew you out of My mouth. Because you say, "I am rich, have become wealthy, and have need of nothing"—and do not know that you are wretched, miserable, poor, blind, and naked (Rev. 3:15-17).

After God points out our great need, He urges: "I counsel you to buy from Me gold refined in the fire, that you may be rich, and white garments, that you may be clothed, that the shame of your nakedness may not be revealed, and anoint your eyes with eye salve, that you may see" (Rev. 3:18).

The gold represents faith and love, and like literal gold, that faith and love gets purified by trials that sometimes seem like fire. The white raiment is Christ's righteousness, and the eye salve represents the ability to discern between good and evil. When thus enriched, clothed, and equipped, we are ready to be used by the Lord.

The opening two verses of Isaiah 66 describe the kind of person for which the King of kings has high regard: one who has "a contrite spirit" and who "trembles" at His Word. The person with a proud heart is highly unlikely to tremble at God's Word. He or she tends to feel little need for the three things that God lists after humility in 2 Chronicles 7:14—earnest prayer, seeking His face, and turning from wickedness.

Contrast

In Proverbs God says, "The fear of the Lord is to hate evil; pride and arrogance and the evil way and the perverse mouth I hate" (Prov. 8:13). As we consider God's loathing of pride, three examples stand out:

- Pride led to Lucifer's fall and changed him into a horrible tyrant (Ezek. 28:17).
- Down through Old Testament history pride blinded the Hebrew leaders

again and again and finally led to the fall of both Israel and Judah.
• The return of Christ could have taken place long before now, but He has had to delay His coming because of the pride within the hearts of many within the ranks of those entrusted with the three angels' messages.

Human nature has a strong tendency to want to feel superior. In an article titled "Feeling 'Superior' Pervasive," the Scrips Howard News service quoted Gordon Allport as saying: "The easiest idea to sell anyone is that he is better that someone else."

A person can even be proud of his or her humility. Or of a supposedly superior form of godliness. The correcting influence, as with so many sins, is "eyes fixed on Jesus" (Hebrews 12:2, TEV). Here's how His example rebukes common examples of pride:

• Pride of birth: "Is not this the carpenter's son?"
• Pride of reputation: "Made Himself of no reputation."
• Pride of financial worth: "The Son of man has not where to lay His head."
• Pride of ability: "I can of my own self do nothing."
• Pride of personal appearance: "He has no form or comeliness."

Elijah's experience

In January 1995, at a presentation I had been asked to make during the ten days of prayer that help start a new year, we examined Elijah's prayer for rain as recorded in 1 Kings 18:42-45. I shared this: When Elijah prayed for fire he got an answer within seconds. But later that same day, as he prayed for rain, no quick answer came. He prayed then sent a servant seven times to see if any clouds were forming out over the Mediterranean before he saw any evidence of an answer. "Why?" asked our prayer group. I then shared something I had earlier found that still amazes and humbles me:

He kept reviewing his life, to see where he had failed to honor God, he confessed his sins, and thus continued to afflict his soul before God, while watching for a token that his prayer was answered.

As he searched his heart, he seemed to be less and less, both in his own estimation and in the sight of God. It seemed to him that he was nothing, and that God was everything; and when he reached the point of renouncing self, while he clung to the Saviour as his only strength and righteousness, the answer came (*SDA Bible Commentary*, Ellen White comments, 2:1035).

Almost every day since that evening I have taken a few minutes before my private morning devotions to do as Elijah did. After a period of reflection I record in my journal, under the heading of "Yesterday," those matters where I had failed to honor God, and ask Him to forgive me.

I am finding that as I gaze on Christ, and especially at Him on the cross, in my mind I become nothing and He becomes everything. As I then bring my requests, I try to cling to Him as my only strength and righteousness. Over the last month, since I started focusing on Matthew 27 and the eight times in that chapter where the blood of Christ is either mentioned or implied, this sense of nothingness has intensified.

Security in Christ's merits

Paul wrote with awesome clarity about righteousness by faith yet confessed that in him there was "nothing good" (Romans 7:18). Romans 8 makes it clear, however, that a sense of our nothingness, of total dependence on Christ, does not destroy self-worth. I see this statement as a central theme of the entire chapter: "As many as are led by the Spirit of God, these are sons of God" (Rom. 8:14).

A son of God. A daughter of God! Romans 8 is filled with references to God's Spirit. Entering into a Spirit-led life brings a sense of worth, of faith, and of courage found nowhere else. That combined with faith in Christ's merits becomes the basis for developing what we mentioned in chapter 2: "unlimited confidence in God."

Still, as least for me, at the start of every day and often through the day, I need a continued awareness that even the slightest inclination toward pride must be melted away by Calvary. Once that becomes widespread in our church, the following will take place: "If we would humble ourselves before God, and be kind and courteous and tenderhearted and pitiful, there would be one hundred conversions to the truth where now there is only one" (*Testimonies for the Church*, 9:189).

More about Elijah

In James 5:17 the apostle reminded us that "Elijah was a man with a nature like ours," or as the New English Bible words it, "a man with human frailties like our own." As that day had developed, Elijah had reasons to feel exultant: (1) the immediate answer to his prayer for fire, (2) the scenes of repentance that had swept through the watching Hebrews, and (3) the swift manner in which his order to destroy the prophets of Baal had been carried out.

Now, as he prayed for rain, it was time for heart-searching and humility. When our prayers are not being answered, we would do well to imitate what Elijah did, as summarized here.

- He didn't give up in discouragement when he got no immediate answer.
- He kept reviewing his life to see where he had failed to honor God.

- He confessed his sins and continued to afflict his soul.
- As he searched his heart, he became less and less in his own eyes and in the eyes of God.
- He reached a point where he saw himself as nothing and God as everything.
- He humbly renounced all of self.
- He clung to Jesus "as his only strength and righteousness."

At that point, the first sign that rain was imminent appeared out over the Mediterranean. He had become humble enough for God to use. And for us today here again is encouragement drawn from the experience of Elijah: "Nothing is apparently more helpless, yet really more invincible, than the soul that feels its nothingness and relies wholly on God" (*Prophets and Kings*, 175).

When I was still eighteen and a new believer, Elder Vandeman said something at a week of prayer at Southwestern Junior College that really helped: "When I look at myself I don't see how I can be saved, but when I look at Jesus I don't see how I could be lost."

Are there ideas you can use in this chapter? May I suggest two possibilities?

- *Write Isaiah 57:15, the above statement from* Prophets and Kings, *and the statement of Elder Vandeman on a 3 by 5 card and keep it with you until you have memorized all three statements.*
- *Each time you start to pray during the next few days, pause to remind yourself that you are clinging to Jesus "as your only strength and righteousness."*

25

Gradualism, Revival, and Seeking God's Face

"O God, You are my God; Early will I seek You; My soul thirsts for You; My flesh longs for You . . . . So I have looked for You in the sanctuary, to see Your power and Your glory" (Ps. 63:1, 2).

Satan has fixed an evil eye on current moves toward revival and is working desperately to block the latter rain from being given. One of his strategies is to get people to adopt a lifestyle that grieves the Holy Spirit. Out of His love for us God has given this warning:

"Do not love the world or the things in the world. If anyone loves the world, the love of the Father is not in him. For all that is in the world—the lust of the flesh, the lust of the eyes, and the pride of life—is not of the Father but is of the world. And the world is passing away, and the lust of it; but he who does the will of God abides forever" (1 John 2:15-17).

The story in Numbers 25 demonstrates how destructive love of the world can be. As Moses worked at getting ready to cross the Jordan into Canaan, most of the Hebrews had free time. They were camped just across from Jericho, in an area where names of some surrounding places suggested sexual thoughts. Moabite women intermingled with the Hebrews under the guise of friendship. Then Moab announced a festival.

Thousands of Hebrews attended. As the festivities progressed "the people seemed to be infatuated. Rulers and the leading men were among the first to transgress, and so many of the people were guilty that the apostasy became national" (*Patriarchs and Prophets,* 454). A plague broke out that slew the 24,000 who had fallen for the Moabite beauties.

Gradualism

The chapter "Apostasy at the Jordan," in *Patriarchs and Prophets*, draws sobering lessons from Numbers 25. Here's one: "Many of the amusements popular in the world today, even among those who claim to be Christians, tend to the same end as those of the heathen. There are indeed few among them that Satan does not turn to account in destroying souls" (459).

A specific technique that Satan uses to entice believers away from a godly lifestyle is *gradualism*—reaching a goal "by gradual stages." Satan used this strategy to erode the power of the early church. A little at a time he got leaders and members to lessen differences between themselves and pagans. "Almost imperceptibly the customs of heathenism found their way into the Christian church" (*The Great Controversy*, 49).

The same thing has happened within much of Protestantism. One time this headline appeared in a St. Louis newspaper: "Pastors Liberalize Stand on Dancing." Previously that denomination had shunned dancing. Then pastors representing eighty congregations decided that dancing was acceptable for young people if properly supervised. The *Adventist Review* editor who reported the incident commented that the time will never come when Adventist pastors make that kind of headline.

He's probably right; no General Conference session will ever approve dancing. Or theater attendance. Or card playing. Or rock music. Or social drinking. Or trashy video entertainment. Yet all of these have become more common among us.

Lifestyle erosions

As examples of the lifestyle erosions currently taking place, consider these two: theater attendance and jewelry.

On a recent Sabbath afternoon several Andrews University students were chatting as they finished an afternoon ministry. "I think I'll go to a movie tonight," one said, and invited others to attend with her. A few years ago, such a thought would have been anathema to students who were involved in sharing their faith.

Earrings, wedding bands, and other kinds of jewelry have also become more common among Adventists, and I can't help but feel that this is a symptom of gradually opening up to the ways of the world. For those who would defend jewelry because it was sometimes worn in the Old Testament, we do well to remember this: Because of the teachings of Jesus the New Testament mandates a higher standard than the Old in several areas. Examples include multiple wives, divorce, and jewelry.

Concerning jewelry 1 Timothy 2:8-10 is clear: no fancy hairdos "or gold or pearls or costly clothing." In his first epistle Peter counseled women in unmistakably clear words that their adornment should be spiritual and internal, rather than the external evidenced by wearing of gold (1 Peter 3:3, 4).

One fall the mother of one of my students was killed in a tragic car-truck accident. To give this precious girl time to recover, I arranged for her to take an incomplete. To discuss her incomplete, I met with her for lunch. She had on what I thought was an engagement ring, so I asked, "Are you engaged?"

"No," she replied, "a girlfriend gave this to me." Then she added, "But I have four friends who are engaged, and all of them are wearing an engagement ring."

Gradualism! Could the relaxation of our stand against outward adornment be one symptom that Satan is leading God's people to depart from New Testament purity and godliness?

Seeking God's face

The third condition for revival given in 2 Chronicles 7:14 is that we seek God's face. David wrote, "When You said, 'Seek My face,' My heart said to You, 'Your face, Lord, I will seek' " (Ps. 27:8). But how does one seek the *face* of God?

In *Transforming Your Prayer Life*, Bob Beltz tells of wondering the same thing. "I began to see," he wrote, "that the concept of the face of God also refers to the nature and character of God. In a sense, all of the attributes and names of God reveal different dimensions of His face" (*Transforming Your Prayer Life* (Dallas, Texas: Word, Inc., 1993), 45).

Pastor Beltz uses the Lord's Prayer in his personal devotions, and in his book devotes a chapter to each of its petitions. In the chapter "Hallowed Be Your Name" he tells his own experience of praying through some of God's names and reflecting on what they mean.

In Jeremiah 23:6, for example, Christ is called "THE LORD OUR RIGHTEOUSNESS." When praying about that name, he thanks God that though he has no righteousness of his own, Jesus died and rose for him and is now the source of his righteousness.

Other names that Beltz uses as he prays include: the Lord who sanctifies (Exod. 31:13), the Lord who is our Shepherd (Ps. 23:1), the Lord who provides (Gen. 22:14), and the Lord who heals (Exod. 15:26). His book led me into a similar use of Bible names as I pray the Lord's Prayer. With the first petition, for example, I pray, "Hallowed be Your name through the righteousness You provide, through the holiness you offer, through Your shepherding of us, etc."

One can add appropriate Bible statements to all six petitions in the Lord's Prayer. As I use that prayer privately, I often mention Christ's blood with each petition: "Through the blood of Christ may Your name be hallowed." In your own prayers never forget that a fervent reference to Christ's blood causes Satan to tremble and flee.

Another life-changing prayer

Along with using three of Paul's prayers, during the summer of 1996 I memorized and now ask students to memorize and use Luke 18:13, "God be merciful to me a sinner" and the following paraphrase from *Christ's Object Lessons:*

> "Lord, take my heart; for I cannot give it. It is Thy property. Keep it pure, for I cannot keep it for thee. Save me in spite of myself, my weak, unchristlike self. Mold me, fashion me, raise me into a pure and holy atmosphere, where the rich current of Thy love can flow through my soul" (159).

In the fall of 1996 I surveyed eighty-five college students about temptation. I listed fifteen proposed chapter titles for a book to be called *Dealing With Temptation.* Their first choice (forty-five of eighty-five) was "My Part and God's Part in Dealing With Temptation." Second highest (forty of eighty-five) was "Tempted to Put Off Getting Ready for Christ's Return." Number three (twenty-three of eighty-five) was "Leaving Out Prayer and Bible Study," and number four (twenty-two of eighty-five) was "Premarital Sex."

Because sex-before-marriage temptations are strong during high school and college years, I have started using the preceding prayer collectively for youth on our 81 college campuses, and our 930 secondary schools. I include myself along with youth as I pray, "Lord, take our hearts, for we cannot give them. . . ."

I came across a questionnaire that asked, "If you had $1,000 in the bank and it cost you $1 every time you thought about sex, how long before you would be broke?" Even Christian young women seem not to realize that wearing abbreviated shorts, split skirts, and miniskirts serves as a temptation to sexual thoughts for many men. As one news reporter has suggested, the sexual nature of many men urges, "See all you can." I have found that in such situations, praying the preceding prayer even once can help dispel the desires of one's carnal nature.

In a chapter in *Steps to Christ* called "The Knowledge of God" Ellen White says this: "God . . . is a lover of the beautiful, and above all that is outwardly attractive He loves beauty of character; He would have us cultivate purity and simplicity, the quiet graces of the flowers" (85).

In this context I again recommend, as Hebrews 12:2 puts it, "Let us keep our eyes fixed on Jesus" (TEV).

Consider two ways to apply this chapter:

- *Read Numbers 25 and the chapter in* Patriarchs and Prophets *titled "Apostasy at the Jordan." What bearing does the latter have upon the story in Numbers 25?*
- *Would you be willing to write the prayer from* Christ's Object Lessons *on a 3 by 5 card and include it in your prayers for Adventist youth everywhere? Be assured of this: every such prayer has a saving and transforming influence on the youthful friends for whom you pray.*

26

Turning From Our Wicked Ways

"Let the wicked forsake his way, and the unrighteous man his thoughts; let him return to the Lord, and He will have mercy upon him; and to our God, for He will abundantly pardon" (Isa. 55:6, 7).

What would you select as the most significant happening of the last 1,000 years? In the fall of 1997, *Life* did a special undated issue that featured what the editors saw as "the 100 most important events of the millennium." Their choice as number one? Gutenberg printing the Bible.

Gutenberg didn't invent printing—that can be traced back to eighth-century China—but *Life* suggested that when he produced 200 gorgeously typeset Bibles in 1455 "he unleashed an information epidemic that rages to this day" (133).

The grace and power found in the Bible are especially important as we look at the fourth thing given in 2 Chronicles 7:14 that helps prepare the way for the latter rain: turning from our wicked ways.

What were the "wicked ways" that held back God's blessings on Judah at the time Isaiah wrote the above statement of Isaiah 55? These included: (1) a form of religion without compassion for hurting people, (2) pride and vanity, (3) idolatry and sexual immorality, and (4) carelessness about the Sabbath.

In the first five chapters of Isaiah the Lord rebukes His people for three of the above four sins, starting in chapter 1 with His people's lack of compassion:

"Even though you make many prayers, I will not hear. . . .
Put away the evil of your doings from before My eyes. Cease to do evil,

learn to do good: seek justice, reprove the oppressor; defend the fatherless, plead for the widow" (Isa. 1:15-17).

People fasted yet exploited their laborers. They prayed but didn't feed the hungry, clothe the naked, or seek to loose the bonds of sin (Isa. 58:6, 7).

Junkyards of idols

After being driven out of Thessalonicia and taken to Athens, Paul sent for Silas and Timothy. "The longer Paul waited in Athens for Silas and Timothy, the angrier he got—all those idols! The city was a junkyard of idols" (Acts 17:16, The Message).

The second chapter of Isaiah told of a similar junkyard in Judah. Isaiah described the land as "full of idols," adding, "They worship the work of their own hands" (Isa. 2:8).

In a comment about the first commandment, *Patriarchs and Prophets* declares: "Man is forbidden to give to any other object the first place in his affections or his service. Whatever we cherish that tends to lessen our love for God or to interfere with the service due Him, of that do we make a god" (305).

How is it with television in our homes? Does it interfere with time for Bible study and for ministry?

The *Chicago Tribune* reported that the average American watches TV for nearly seven hours a day. The *Tribune* told of a poll in which one-fourth of the adults queried said they would not give up their TV if offered a million dollars for doing so! Could TV be one of the "junkyard" idols in many of our homes?

With God's help my wife and I raised three children without getting a TV set. Now two of the three are raising their children the same way. The advantages have been many: more time for outdoor activities, more closeness as a family, a greater interest in reading, and the shutting out of much evil.

Pride and wantonness

Isaiah 3 notes that along with oppressing the poor (13-15) people were imitating the ungodly styles of their neighbors. Isaiah described the daughters of Zion as "haughty"—walking "with outstretched necks and wanton eyes . . . mincing as they go, making a jingling with their feet" (16, 17).

The prophet gets specific—he mentions bracelets, leg ornaments, earrings, nose jewels, and a dozen other kinds of ornaments and fancy dress (Isa. 3:18-23, KJV). Most were designed to call attention to the wearer, though items such as purses and mirrors (22, 23, NKJV) do have a practical use.

Most people ignored Isaiah's reproofs. In *The Bible as History*, Werner

Keller reports: "However much the prophets railed against it they were never able to drive the ancient equivalents of rouge and mascara completely out of the boudoirs of the wealthy" (*The Bible as History* [New York: Bantam Books, 1982], 235). The Hebrews were influenced by the Egyptians and Canaanites, who used a lot of cosmetics and wore earrings, beads, rings, armbands, and bracelets.

These things make Paul's advice in Romans 12:1, 2 doubly powerful: "Present your bodies a living sacrifice, holy, acceptable to God . . . and do not be conformed to the world, but be transformed by the renewing of your mind."

Battling idolatry

When they entered the Promised Land, the Hebrews did not expel heathen tribes as God had ordered. The results from mingling with and marrying the ungodly were horrible. "Then the children of Israel did evil in the sight of the Lord, and served the Baals; and they forsook the Lord God of their fathers . . . and they followed other gods . . . and they bowed down to them" (Judges 2:11, 12).

During Samuel's leadership some reforms took place, but the people became weary of a simple lifestyle and pleaded for a king, "that we also may be like all the nations" (1 Sam. 8:20). After the death of Solomon and the division of the nation, Rehoboam ruled Judah for nineteen years. During his reign idolatry rapidly increased. "They did according to all the abominations of the nations" (1 Kings 14:24).

Isaiah repeatedly pointed out the folly of worshiping things made by human hands (Isa. 40:18-31; 41:21-29; 57:1-13). For us today, contrast the amounts spent on luxuries with what we invest in kingdom needs. As with his contemporaries, Paul would urge, "Flee from idolatry" (1 Cor. 10:14).

Simplicity and godliness

If you were to list lifestyle characteristics found in Christ as seen in the Gospels, what would you include? Courtesy? Compassion for people? Simplicity? Cheerfulness and tact? Graciousness? Consistency? Purity?

For those who want to imitate Him, *Gospel Workers* offers this advice:

"The religion of Jesus softens whatever is hard and rough in the temper, and smooths whatever is rugged and sharp in the manners. It makes the words gentle and the demeanor winning. Let us learn from Christ how to combine a high sense of purity and integrity with sunniness of disposition" (122).

Don't you love such a person? "A kind, courteous Christian is the most powerful argument that can be produced in favor of Christianity" (ibid.).

Simplicity and godliness affect every part of life. Take the homes we build for ourselves. Since the early 1900s our families have decreased in size from up to a dozen or more children to just over two children in the average family. At the same time we have been building bigger and still bigger houses.

What might be the benefits to God's work if all Adventists were content with a simple lifestyle in which a passion for possessions and luxuries was replaced with passion for Christ and for winning people to Him? If every dollar thus saved was invested in organizations like ADRA and Adventist World Radio, the amount given could total scores of millions of dollars every year. With God's blessing, couldn't these extra funds help produce millions of additional converts?

Temples for Christ

Romans 12:1, 2—give your body and mind to God—makes faith very practical. The fact that God designed our bodies to be temples for the Holy Spirit (1 Cor. 6:19, 20) also gives a certain sacredness to the body *and* to the mind. The desire to sin, or the desire to be godly, originate in the mind. That's why Paul urges that we bring "every thought into captivity" to Christ, or as the New English Bible words it, "compel every human thought to surrender in obedience to Christ" (2 Cor. 10:5).

And what does that include? A. G. Daniells put it like this: "Surrender means the uttermost giving up of all that we have and are to the mastery of Jesus—our worst, our best, our possessions, our past, our future, our life plans, our loved ones, our will, our *self.* That is surrender" (cited in May Cole Kuhn, *A Leader of Men* (Washington, DC: Review and Herald, 1946), 91).

That kind of surrender "greatly simplifies the problem of life. It weakens and cuts short a thousand struggles with the passions of the natural heart" (*Messages to Young People*, 30).

Here's another new prayer habit I'm working to develop: When meeting a young person, or a group of them, I try to send up a prayer to God that each one will recognize his or her body as a temple for the Holy Spirit. In doing so I try to see people not as they are, but as they can become through Christ.

- *Jesus told Satan, "Man shall not live by bread alone, but by every word which proceeds from the mouth of God" (Matt. 4:4). What significance do you see in the expression "every word"? How does that apply to the content of this chapter?*
- *Are you ready to try another new prayer habit? Think of each young person in your local church as potentially a godly temple for the Holy Spirit. On Sabbaths, and during the week, too, ask God to make each one a Christ-filled temple.*

27

Compassion, the Sabbath, and Prosperity

**"Those who honor Me I will honor,
and those who despise Me
shall be lightly esteemed" (1 Sam. 2:30).**

Did you know that Isaiah 58 contains three of the most full-of-wonder promises in all the Bible?

The opening verses rebuke the people of Judah for a religion of form in which there was no compassion for people. God next tells the kind of "fasts" He wants: loosing bonds of wickedness, undoing heavy burdens, freeing the oppressed, sharing bread, and clothing the naked. Then comes the first of three promises: "Then your light shall break forth like the morning, your healing shall spring forth speedily. . . . Then you shall call, and the Lord will answer; you shall cry, and He will say, 'Here I am' " (Isa. 58:8, 9).

Through Isaiah God again mentions helping the hungry and the afflicted and makes another promise: "Then your light shall dawn in the darkness, and your darkness shall be as noonday. . . . You shall be like a watered garden, and like a spring of water whose waters do not fail" (Isa. 58:10, 11).

What an offer! Even in experiences that could bring gloom, that gloom will become "as noonday" and you will be like "a spring of water whose waters do not fail."

A century ago Ellen White wrote that the work we are to do as a church "is outlined in the fifty-eighth chapter of Isaiah" (*The Upward Look*, 360). Do you see the applications? First help people with material needs and with your friendship, and when possible invite them to your home for a meal. Within the charm of your friendship many will respond to invitations to hear the gospel.

Compassion tries to help with physical needs, but godly compassion also takes note of spiritual needs and seeks to share the healing found only in Jesus. No one is fully provided for until he or she understands how to find freedom from the bad habits of a life of sin.

Christ modeled the compassion enjoined in Isaiah 58. He "went about doing good" (Acts 10:38). "His compassion knew no limit" (*Gospel Workers*, 41).

Sabbath as a delight

During Isaiah's time the people of Judah had become careless about Sabbath observance. "If you keep the Sabbath holy," God told them, "not having your own fun and business on that day, but enjoying the Sabbath and speaking of it with delight as the Lord's holy day, and honoring the Lord in what you do, not following your own desires and pleasure, nor talking idly—then the Lord will be your delight, and I will see to it that you ride high, and get your full share of the blessings I promised to Jacob, your father. The Lord has spoken" (Isa. 58:13, 15, TLB).

"I will see to it that you . . . get your full share of blessings I promised to Jacob—that's the third promise of Isaiah 58.

Note the condition for getting a "full share" of God's blessings: seeking delight in God and in His Sabbath. That delight excludes secular business and conversation on the Sabbath, and secular games.

Heaven's "full share of blessings" was repeatedly promised to Israel. In Deuteronomy 5, God had Moses give the Ten Commandments to the people a second time. In that oration Moses repeatedly spoke of God's desire that things "may be well" with them (Deut. 5:32, 33; 6:18; 12:28). The context offered rich blessings: spiritual excellence, material wealth, social harmony, physical vigor, and godly children.

The Hebrew people never got the "full share" of these blessings. Does carelessness about Sabbath preparation and observance also rob us of many blessings?

Finding delight in the Sabbath begins with finding delight in God. It's love for Him that markedly increases the joy we find in spending Sabbath time with Him.

When I first dated the girl at Union College who eventually became my wife, school rules required fellows and girls to use separate cafeteria lines. A hostess told you where to sit. But Tuesday night was date night: we could go through line together and eat together. That was a precious time for us both!

Let's suppose that on those special Tuesday nights I took my college algebra book along. Then as I ate I worked on algebra instead of visiting with my date. Wouldn't that have ruined the specialness for both of us?

Do you see a parallel with Sabbath specialness? It's as we find delight in the Lord that the Sabbath becomes a delight. We will no more talk about weekday matters or play weekday games than I would work algebra at our Tuesday night supper date.

God is eager to give His remnant people their "full share" of blessings. "Every deliverance, every blessing, that God in the past has granted His people, should be kept fresh in memory's hall as a sure pledge of further and richer, increasing blessings that He will bestow. There is no limit to the blessings that it is our privilege to receive" (*Our High Calling*, 196).

"*A sure pledge!*" Be encouraged, also, with this: "Reformations will take place . . . for the divine agencies are efficient to enlighten and sanctify the human understanding (*Our Father Cares*, 237). And as reformation occurs, expect this: "Through most wonderful workings of God, mountains of difficulty will be removed and cast into the sea" (ibid., 238).

Press together! Press together!

In his attempt to fragment the church Satan has used prejudice, liberalism, dissidents, attempted date-setting, rejection of authority, generational differences, and other evils. But if as a church body we used the Sabbath for the joyous purposes God designed it—family time, worship, fellowship, and ministry—a wonderful bonding would take place.

Note what the author of Acts wrote about how cohesion and church growth took place after 3,000 had been baptized on the Day of Pentecost:

> And they continued steadfastly in the apostles' doctrine and fellowship, in the breaking of bread, and in prayers. . . . Continuing daily with one accord in the temple, and breaking bread from house to house, they ate their food with gladness and simplicity of heart, praising God and having favor with all the people. And the Lord added to the church daily those who were being saved (Acts 2: 42, 46, 47).

In Jesus' prayer, recorded in John 17, He prayed for our oneness. "I do not pray for these alone," He said, "but also for those who will believe in Me through their word; that they all may be one, as You, Father, are in Me, and I in You; that they also may be one in Us, that the world may believe You sent Me" (John 17:20, 21).

Recently I checked the CD-ROM that contains all of the published writings of Ellen White. I found that the phrase "press together" occurs forty-three times. Note the concern she expressed at the General Conference meetings in 1901:

> "There seems to be in this meeting an endeavor to press together. This is the word which for the last fifty years I have heard from the

angelic hosts—press together, press together. Let us try to do this. When in the spirit of Jesus we try to press together, putting ourselves out of sight, we shall find that the Holy Spirit will come in, and the blessing of God will rest upon us" (cited in *Ellen G. White*, 5:89).

Sometimes the expression "press together" was consecutively repeated four times. In one paragraph of words spoken at the above meetings, she used "press together" five times in five sentences (*Selected Messages*, 2:374).

Then in the next paragraph she added, "I repeat the message to you. As you go to your homes, be determined that you will press together; seek God with all the heart, and you will find Him, and the love of Christ that passeth understanding, will come into your hearts and lives" (ibid., 374, 375).

Seeking the Lord and seeking humility must merge. "Seek the Lord, all you meek of the earth. . . . Seek righteousness, seek humility" (Zeph. 2:3).

What God said through Zephaniah takes us right back to 2 Chronicles 7:14, where the first requirement for rain and blessing is that we humble ourselves. As just mentioned, self must be put "out of sight."

Let's use the Sabbath to help bring about the unity that Jesus prayed for in John 17: "that . . . all may be one" (21).

- *Could I recommend a book filled with practical ideas that helps make preparation for the Sabbath much easier? It's Yara Coria Young's* Oh No, It's Sabbath Again, and I'm Not Ready, *published by Pacific Press®.*
- *Volume 6 of* Testimonies for the Church *contains a chapter titled "The Observance of the Sabbath" that richly blessed our family as our children were growing up. Read it together as husband and wife; then take several Sabbaths to share ideas from it on Saturday evenings and get input from your children as to how you as a family can "remember" the Sabbath all week long.*

28

Obsessed, Possessed, and Blessed

"In the beginning was the Word, and the Word was with God, and the Word was God. . . . And the Word became flesh and dwelt among us, and we beheld His glory, the glory as of the only begotten of the Father, full of grace and truth" (John 1:1, 14).

A young woman who came to Christ through the *Voice of Prophecy* wrote, "Through Christ I went from a *nobody* to a *somebody.*" In Luke 15 Jesus repeatedly tried to show how precious people are to Him. These parables—the lost sheep, the lost coin, and lost son—illustrate the fact that you will never meet a person who doesn't matter to God.

Men such as Caesar, Nero, and Hitler sacrificed millions of their own people in order to carry out their selfish ambitions. Thomas Campbell, Scottish poet, exclaimed, "What millions died—that Caesar might be great!"

Contrast that with the above passage from John 1. Of Jesus we can say, "*He* died—that millions might be great!"

As a comment on the story of Christ's birth consider this: "In contemplating the incarnation of Christ in humanity, we stand baffled before an unfathomable mystery, that the human mind cannot comprehend. The more we reflect upon it, the more amazing does it appear" (*Seventh-day Adventist Bible Commentary,* 5: 1130).

The word *Incarnation* means "in the flesh." We can't grasp the wonder of it, but the more we reflect, the more amazing it appears!

That's the purpose of this chapter—to experience that sense of amazement at who Christ is and what He has done.

Youth and the Incarnation

In our academy religion texts we had a nine-week unit based on the first half of Matthew. The lesson about Matthew 1 began with several paragraphs about the vastness of God's galactic empire. For artwork Howie Larkin, the art director at Pacific Press, used a painting of two galaxies passing through each other. Space is so vast that galaxies can do that with no danger of collisions.

The average size of a galaxy like the Milky Way is *100 billion suns*. If you had inherited *just one billion* dollars at the time of Christ and had spent one thousand dollars a day ever since, you'd still have enough left to keep on spending one thousand dollars a day for more than seven hundred years!

That's just one billion! Beyond our own there are hundreds of billions of other galaxies. These galaxies are in clusters, with our own cluster of about thirty galaxies called the Local Group. That is a *small* cluster; one cluster in the Coma constellation has 10,000 galaxies.

Astronomers claim these clusters are arranged into superclusters. Some believe that the superclusters probably are arranged into clusters of super superclusters.

After we had had class discussion I sought student feedback and asked them to write a short answer to this question: "Do you see the Incarnation as something that awakens more love for Jesus? And if so, why?"

The majority answered Yes; here's a sample of their replies as to why:

Scott: "I can't understand why Jesus, who controls billions and billions of galaxies, would come down to one tiny world and die for me."

Alisa: "A great king or president wouldn't give up his position to become a street cleaner. For anyone as great as Christ to come down as a baby so He could grow up and die for us is wonderful."

Tom: "If Jesus hadn't come, there would be no hope for tomorrow."

Lorena: "I realize more and more how much Jesus loved me and what He gave up to save me."

Tony: "What Jesus did would be like a human being turning into a small germ and staying that way forever."

Gad: "For the Maker of all the stars to become a tiny baby in Mary's arms is unfathomable."

An intergalactic goodbye

Unfathomable. Let's try to make it more real. At a point nine months before the birth of Christ, Jesus our Creator ceased to be except as a tiny cell to be implanted in the womb of a teenage girl named Mary. Don't you think the Father and Holy Spirit must have said goodbye to Christ just before He was transformed into a sperm cell? How did they spend their last hour together? What did they say to each other?

No intergalactic news reporter was present to do a story, but in my mind I see the Father embracing the Son and clinging to Him a really long time. He may then have said something like this: "Thank You, Son, for taking this risk. It gives us a chance to save some really precious people and the universe itself. I love You, and I'll be thinking about You constantly and watching over You."

I picture the Holy Spirit also embracing Christ then taking His hand to tell Him, "Angels will be constantly watching over You. My love will surround You every moment."

What happened next? Possibly a bright light surrounded our Saviour, or a cloud, and somehow He became a tiny sperm. The Bible simply says, "The Word became flesh" (John 1:14). He was nurtured in Mary's womb for nine months and then born in the same manner as each of us.

A reason for astonishment

Christ's personality gives us another reason for wonder. Isaiah had predicted, "His name shall be called Wonderful" (Isa. 9:6, KJV). Webster defines *wonder* as a reason for astonishment, a cause for amazed admiration, something not previously known.

A reason for astonishment. In closing his Gospel, John used this hyperbole: If all Jesus had done were written, "even the world itself could not contain the books" (John 21:25). And in eternity it will be "still more and more" forever!

Cause for amazed admiration. Jesus Christ speaks worlds and galaxies into existence "with the breath of His mouth" (Ps. 33:6). He guides clusters and superclusters of galaxies on their sweep through space! Yet He has condescended to take human form for all ages to come—and thinks of us as "brethren" (Heb. 2:11).

Something beyond anything previously known. As humans, we want friends—and a spouse—who are considerate, congenial, and compatible. Jesus is all that—a thousand times over. He has every likable quality in the dictionary.

Obsessed, possessed, blessed

The word *obsession*, in a negative sense, has to do with being controlled by an evil spirit. In today's society people become obsessed with a lot of things just as hurtful as an evil spirit—alcohol, status seeking, power seeking, making money, excessive TV watching, and an idolatrous interest in sports. To that we could add obsessions less hurtful but not good: ice cream, fried chicken, bedtime snacks, etc.

On the positive side, *obsession* can mean becoming totally engrossed with an idea or desire—like getting the gospel to "every nation, tribe, tongue, and people" (Rev. 14:6). I want to suggest that we also have every right to become obsessed with Jesus Christ.

That, in turn, enables us to become *possessed* by God's Spirit. The more possessed we become, the more Philippians 2:5 becomes our desire, "Let this mind be in you, which was also in Christ Jesus" (Phil. 2:5). We yearn to be "filled with the fruits of righteousness" (Phil. 1:11).

We are then truly *blessed* with the "abundant" life Jesus promised in John 10:10. God fulfills for us a promise He made to Abraham: "I'll bless you with everything I have—bless and bless and bless!" (Heb. 6:14, The Message).

From this chapter content why not try one of the following?

- *Cruden's Concordance(to the KJV) lists 140 different titles or names for Jesus Christ, such as Captain (Heb. 2:10), King of Kings (Rev.19:16), Lamb of God (John 1:29), Living Water (John 4:10), Morning Star (Rev.22:16), and Servant (Isa.42:1). A name often suggests a character quality. Captain, for example, implies competence, leadership skills, excellence. Take a little Bible-study time and make a list of possible character qualities you find in the preceding six names or titles.*
- *At the bottom of the first page in most* The Desire of Ages *chapters you will find the Bible texts with which that chapter deals. Select a chapter in the* The Desire of Ages, *look up and read the scripture listed, and then the chapter. After each reading, write or mentally note admirable traits of Jesus.*

29

The Power of Christ's Healing Love

"And when Jesus went out He saw a great multitude; and He was moved with compassion for them, and healed their sick" (Matt. 14:14).

If you were a fourteen-year-old who had decided for Christ and baptism, would you go to the man who had helped murder your father and ask him to be the officiating pastor? Stephen made that choice, as did his sister Cathy.

Stephen and Cathy were children of Nate Saint, one of five American missionaries who were killed by Waorani Indians in 1955. But one day, just a few years later, as the sun rose on a sandbar in the Ecuador's Curaray River, Steve and Cathy stood together listening to Kimo, a Waorani pastor, explain the meaning of baptism. In 1955, Kimo had been one of the warriors who killed the missionaries on this very sandbar. Then the pastor baptized Nate's two children.

What had made the change in this man? The families of the slain missionaries did not flee Ecuador. In fact, Nate's sister Rachel, along with Elizabeth Elliott, the widow of one of the other men, continued to work with a Waorani woman who had left her village. Eventually that woman was able to return to her home and persuade the villagers to allow Rachel and Elizabeth to come to the village.

Rachel and Elizabeth lived their forgiveness in the Indian village. Kimo was one of the first to come to Christ. And Steve and Cathy chose him to conduct their baptism.

Our compassionate Saviour

The statement with which we began this lesson speaks of Christ being *moved* with compassion. In an attempt to get away from the crowds, Jesus and His disciples had left Capernaum and gone by boat across to the east side of Galilee. But even there they were met by a large crowd.

Several years ago I read from a set of Ellen White books called *The Spirit of Prophecy*—the forerunners of the Conflict of the Ages set. Volume 2 deals with the life of Christ and contains interesting details not mentioned in *The Desire of Ages.*

One such detail is this: "Hundreds" of afflicted people had been laid out on the beach to await His coming. "There were the deaf, the blind, the palsied, the lame, and lunatic. In looking upon this wretched throng the heart of Jesus melted with compassion" (2:259).

That describes Jesus—a heart that *melted* for hurting people and that tenderly loved the most erring. The opening page of *The Ministry of Healing* puts it like this: "His compassion knew no limit" (17).

Jesus had hoped for rest and became so weary that as the afternoon wore on some of the disciples feared He would die of fatigue. "Peter and John each took an arm of their beloved Master and kindly endeavored to draw Him away. But He refused to be moved from the place" (*Spirit of Prophecy*, 2:260, 261).

Later in the afternoon, Jesus beckoned for Peter to bring a boat, and He taught from it for a while. Then as the sun moved toward the western horizon, He worked the miracle of the loaves and fishes. The people were so impressed that they determined to proclaim Him king right on the spot.

Matthew says, "Immediately Jesus made His disciples get into the boat and go before Him to the other side, while He sent the multitudes away. And when He had sent the multitudes away, He went up on a mountain by Himself to pray. And when evening had come, He was alone there" (Matt. 14:23). Jesus knew that the reaction of the priests in an attempt to crown Him would have shortened His ministry, so He quietly ordered the crowd to leave.

Even though fatigued, Jesus felt a burden to pray. With the crowd and disciples gone, He goes to His knees in prayer. The closing two paragraphs of "The Loaves and Fishes" chapter tell of His compassion for the people and then describe His prayer time. He apparently prayed for hours, because the disciples, caught in a storm, had to labor at their oars for "hour after hour" (ibid., 267).

The final paragraph of the chapter mentions His "tears and strong cries for his mistaken people." If I could have been in the shadows to listen as Jesus prayed, I think I probably would have also wept. Note this sentence: "Deep emotion shakes that noble form as he keenly realizes the doom of the people he has come to save" (ibid.).

What will it take?

"And I, if I am lifted up from the earth, will draw all peoples to myself,"

Jesus said (John 12:32). "The goodness of God," wrote Paul, "leads you to repentance" (Rom. 2:4).

Many of the 120 people mentioned in Acts 1, who met in the upper room to pray, had been at Calvary. During their time in the upper room, their memories of Calvary led to deep heart searching. The Holy Spirit hovered over them. As they sensed that Presence, they:

- Repeated to one another the truths Jesus had taught
- Humbled their hearts, grieved for their dullness, and confessed their unbelief
- Put away all differences, all desire for supremacy, and came close together in Christian fellowship
- Developed an intense concern for lost people
- Pleaded with God to fill them with His Spirit

What would it take for the preceding scenes to be repeated? Consider the following appeal:

"One member working in right lines will lead other members to unite with him in making intercession for the revelation of the Holy Spirit. . . .There will be no confusion, because all will be in harmony with the mind of the Spirit. The barriers separating believer from believer will be broken down, and God's servants will speak the same things. The Lord will co-operate with His servants. All will pray understandingly the prayer that Christ taught His servants, 'Thy kingdom come. Thy will be done in earth, as it is in heaven.' Matthew 6:10" (*Testimonies for the Church*, 8:251).

One member working in right lines. What are these "right lines"?

One could be small groups that meet weekly to study and pray together. Here's one possible format: Use suggestions in chapter 13 and read and discuss parts of Isaiah 53. For several meetings thereafter, focus on the last chapters of one of the Gospels or the *The Desire of Ages* chapter entitled "Calvary."

God is able "to do exceedingly abundantly above all that we ask or think, according to the power that works in us" (Eph. 3:20). Let's do "whatever it takes" to help bring about the fulfillment of the latter rain promises given in Joel 2. When that happens, God will remove every barrier, and our crucified Saviour will be lifted up "in every nation, tribe, tongue, and people" (Rev. 14:6).

Writing this chapter has moved me deeply. Could I make a suggestion that might help you experience something similar?

- *The story of the feeding of the 5,000 is found in* The Desire of Ages *under the title "Give Ye Them to Eat." First read Matthew 14:13-21 and then the account in* The Desire of Ages. *As you read keep asking, "What is there to see? What is there to hear? What is there to feel?"*
- *If you have access to volume 2 of* The Spirit of Prophecy, *read the chapter called "The Loaves and the Fishes." As already noted, it contains some pen pictures not found in* The Desire of Ages. *Portions of it may bring tears to your eyes.*

30

Ankle Deep, Knee Deep . . .

**"Then . . . he brought me through the waters;
the water came up to my ankles" (Ezek. 47:3).**

Ezekiel 43 to 46 describe a temple that could have become the source for healing waters that would have flowed out to Israel's neighbors with all kinds of blessings. Then Ezekiel 47 tells of an angel who took Ezekiel in vision to a gate on the east side of that future temple and showed him a small stream of water that flowed out on the south side of the entrance. The angel measured off one thousand cubits, or 1,500 feet, and they both waded across ankle deep water, after which:

"Again he measured one thousand and brought me through the waters; the water came up to my knees. Again he measured one thousand and brought me through; the water came up to my waist. Again he measured one thousand, and it was a river I could not cross, for the water was too deep" (Ezek. 47:4, 5).

The river flowed into the Dead Sea, bringing healing all along the way. Trees along the river bore fruit every month, with leaves that were to be used for medicine.

With Israel, unbelief and disobedience frustrated God's plan, but today the three angels' messages are taking the healing stream of the everlasting gospel to the ends of the earth.

"Read Ezekiel 47"

In volume 7 of the *Testimonies for the Church*, penned in 1902, Ellen

White wrote: "Our work has been presented to me as, in its beginning, a small, very small, rivulet." She then goes on to say:

> "Read Ezekiel 47. Especially mark verse 8: 'Then he said unto me, These waters issue out toward the east country, and go down into the desert, and go into the sea: which being brought forth into the sea, the waters shall be healed.' So our work was presented to me as extending to the east and to the west, to the islands of the sea, and to all parts of the world" (*Testimonies for the Church,* 7:171, 172).

All parts of the world parallels this Revelation 14:6 statement: "Then I saw another angel flying in the midst of heaven, having the everlasting gospel to preach to those who dwell on the earth—to every nation, tribe, tongue, and people" (Rev. 14:6).

In the fall of 1995, as I returned from a week of prayer at Grants Pass, Oregon, clouds obscured the ground much of the way to Chicago. Then shortly before we crossed the Mississippi River all the clouds disappeared. Across Illinois and into Chicago sunshine flooded the landscape. I had a window seat and could see every town, every farmhouse. As I looked down I thought of this prediction: "I saw another angel coming down from heaven, having great authority, and the earth was illuminated with his glory" (Rev. 18:1).

I compared what I could see below with the word *illuminated.* When that prophecy is fulfilled, no city or town will be excluded.

Light to every city and town

In the 1980s, when working on academy religion texts, my job included developing a nine-week unit based on Revelation. As I looked for statements that would enlarge on Revelation 18:1, I came across this: "Light will be communicated to every city and town. The earth will be filled with the knowledge of salvation. So abundantly will the renewing Spirit of God have crowned with success the intensely active agencies that the light of present truth will be seen flashing everywhere" (*Evangelism,* 694).

Every city and town in North Korea! Every city and town in Iran, Turkey, and Saudi Arabia! Every community in India and Pakistan! Every city and town in secular Australia, Western Europe, and North America. *The light of present truth flashes everywhere*!

We chose "The Loud Cry" as a title for the lesson that dealt with Revelation 18. I began the lesson by asking students, "Do you ever pray, alone or in a group, for the outpouring of the Holy Spirit? Do such prayers do any good?"

I mentioned that Christ asked us to pray especially for the Holy Spirit (Luke 11:13). As I worked on the narrative part of the lesson I came across this incredible statement:

When the third angel's message shall go forth with a loud voice, the whole earth shall be lightened with His glory, the Holy Spirit is poured out upon His people. The revenue of glory has been accumulating for this closing work of the Third Angel's Message. The prayers that have been ascending for the fulfillment of the promise—the descent of the Holy Spirit—not one has been lost. Each prayer has been accumulating, ready to overflow and pour forth a healing flood of heavenly influence and accumulated light all over the world" (*Manuscript Releases*, 21:155).

Not one prayer lost. Have you been praying ongoing prayers for the latter rain? Not one earnest, fervent prayer of the last 150 years has been lost. Not one of yours will be lost either.

Enlarge! Lengthen! Strengthen!

Under the symbolism of a tent that needs to be enlarged, Isaiah gave this commission: "Enlarge the place of your tent, and let them stretch out the curtains of your habitations; do not spare; lengthen your cords, and strengthen your stakes. For you shall expand to the right and to the left" (Isa. 54:2, 3).

The same page that assures us that not one prayer for the latter rain is lost tells the results: "New victories, under the love and grace of Jesus Christ, are to be added to the domains of the church. The barren places of earth will become as the garden of the Lord" (*Manuscript Releases*, 21:155).

Barren places will become as the garden of the Lord. Few places are as barren of Christianity as North Korea or places like Iran and Saudi Arabia. Impossible as it seems, even these lands will become *as the garden of the Lord.*

Isaiah speaks to prayer warriors on the walls of Jerusalem and commissions them: "You who make mention of the Lord, do not keep silent, and give Him no rest till He establishes and till He makes Jerusalem a praise in the earth" (Isa. 62:6, 7).

As we pray, let's open our Bibles to Joel 2 and ask God to give us the repentance urged in verses 12-17. Join me, if God so leads, in praying with the earnestness the chapter "Praying With Intensity" describes.

Here are additional suggestions:

- *Our church is divided into ninety-two unions. These unions contain a total of 443 conferences and missions. Be encouraged by this: Every prayer for the Holy Spirit has been accumulating, and in the latter rain a flood of light will go everywhere.*
- *Do you ever pray aloud? In Luke 11:1, when the disciples asked, "Lord, teach us to pray," Jesus was praying aloud in the out-of-doors.* Our High Calling *contains this suggestion: "Learn to pray aloud where only God can hear you."(124). Why not find an out-of-doors place where you can be alone and pray aloud from time to time? Perhaps this week you could especially pray for all Adventist youth.*

Postscript

In this book an ongoing theme has been to seek more and more and still more of God's blessings. I want to close with a testimony about the things I long for God to do in my own life in the months ahead. The blessings you most desire may differ, but perhaps you can use the following as a starter for a list of your own. Here's what I pray God will continue to give me:

1. A growing desire for "still more and more" of everything God offers.
In Philippians 1:9-11 Paul asked God to give the Philippians the love that abounds "still more and more in knowledge and all discernment." As I seek more and more of Christ, I praise God that "there is no difficulty within or without that cannot be surmounted in His strength" and that "trustful dependence on Jesus makes victory not only possible, but certain" (*In Heavenly Places*, 17).

2. A deeper awareness of the fact that God eagerly waits for His children to come to Him in prayer.
Wesley Duewel, as cited in chapter 4, puts it like this: "Approach the throne with eager joy. You are asking for things God longs to do. . . . Your prayer time is always a joy time to the Lord" (*Mighty Prevailing Prayer*, 46).

3. An ever-increasing gratitude for the righteousness of Christ—a blessing which means that in intercessory prayer I can enter God's presence clothed with Christ's priestly garments.

In Zechariah 3, when Joshua the High Priest stood before the Lord in filthy garments, Satan stood there as his accuser. Jesus rebuked Satan and put His own robe on Joshua. I praise God that Jesus offers repentant sinners that same blessing.

4. Awareness that Satan trembles and flees when I claim the blood of

Christ in intercessory prayer for those on my prayer list.

I see this as the most powerful argument any of us could ever use as we ask God to work with power in the worldwide work of the three angels' messages.

5. Gratitude for the fact that when we intercede for others, angels minister to them.

Paul mentions the ministry of heavenly angels in Hebrews 1:14. In chapter 6 we included the fact that when we pray for the sick, angels do a ministry "in response to [our] petitions" that otherwise they would not do (*Medical Ministry*, 195).

Logic suggests that a similar ministry is performed by angels when we pray for the spiritually ill—the discouraged, the lukewarm, the indifferent.

6. A growing confidence that it is part of God's plan to grant us, in answer to prayers of faith, blessings He would not give if we didn't ask.

"Ask, and it will be given to you," Jesus told the disciples and us (Luke 11:9). That implies we lose a lot when we don't ask, and lets me know that prayer—my prayers—can really make a difference.

7. An ever-deepening conviction that as I pray for Adventist youth God can and will work wonderful transformations in their young lives.

When Peter wrote about being "kept by the power of God through faith for salvation ready to be revealed," he used a Greek military word, *kept*, that means "garrisoned" (1 Peter 1:5). Thus as I open my Bible to 1 Peter and ask God to send garrisons of angels to surround the youth whom I know and the millions I don't know, God eagerly takes my request and goes into action.

8. Thankfulness that as I bring big requests to God, He has all the mental capacity He needs to handle them.

Our educational system has 81 colleges or universities, 930 academies, and more than 4500 elementary schools (about 900,000 students). Scripture twice says that God calls every star by name (Isa. 40:26; Ps. 147:4). If you or I ask Jesus to place the name of every young Seventh-day Adventist on the palm of His hand, and bless them accordingly, He gladly does so. He loves to have His people bring big requests.

9. Under the guidance of the Holy Spirit I want an ever-increasing love for seekers everywhere who do not yet know Christ.

In chapter 7 we related the experience of Julie Hill, a senior nursing student at PUC, in using Philippians 1:9-11 in behalf of the girls on her floor of the girls' dorm. During the summer of 1997, Julie served as director for seventeen youth working as literature evangelists in Seattle, Washington. Here's another experience she shared with me:

"At one house two children answered the door, and I asked for their mother. When the mother came to the door, several other children came with her. As I showed her *God's Answers to Your Questions*, a ten-year-old daughter took the book and clasped it to her breast.

"Her mother exclaimed, 'I knew she would want it. She has visited seven different churches. She said she is looking for one that teaches the Bible.' This girl went and got ten $1 bills and paid me for the book."

As I mentioned in chapter 10, I have turned again and again to Isaiah 49 in praying for children. Nearly one-third of earth's six billion people are under the age of fifteen. Among them there must be millions who, if they could only know about Jesus, would love Him. May God help me not to go through a single day without sending up prayers in their behalf.

10. I want an ever closer fellowship with the Holy Spirit.

"Let's pray as we walk," Delinda said, catching up with me as I walked toward an auditorium where she, Philip, and myself had been asked to conduct a Concert of Prayer. I had done prayer walks before, but that was the first time a student had suggested praying while walking to an appointment.

A Lake Union Youth Leadership Training Conference had begun earlier that day, and the Concert of Prayer was to be one of the options that people could attend after the general session. About twenty-five youth leaders chose to attend. Along with testimonies, Philip and Delinda shared some of the "how to" suggestions found in chapter 13 of this book. Both of them led their groups into Bible study and prayer.

For the study each used the story of the persistent widow and unjust judge in Luke 18. Delinda and Philip's enthusiasm for Christ and for the Bible were so contagious that at the close, two different individuals asked for a weekend prayer conference at their home churches. As I divided time between both groups, memory brought to mind this statement:

> "With such an army of workers as our youth, rightly trained, might furnish, how soon the message of a crucified, risen, and soon-coming Saviour might be carried to the whole world! How soon might the end come—the end of suffering and sorrow and sin! (*Education*, 271).

As the three of us held a short debriefing at the close, both Delinda and Philip commented about the powerful sense of the Holy Spirit's presence. "God wonderfully answered our prayers," Delinda said. For the participants and for us the evening had been a foretaste of heaven.

May God multiply such experiences for every young person in His church, and for all of us!